MW01041647

DREAMING ALOUD

The Life and Films
of James Cameron

Christopher Heard

Doubleday Canada Limited

Copyright © 1997 Christopher Heard
Revised edition 1998

All rights reserved. No part of this publication may be reproduced, stored
in a retrieval system or transmitted, in any form, or by any means, electronic,
mechanical, photocopying, recording or otherwise, without the prior written
permission of Doubleday Canada Limited.

Canadian Cataloguing in Publication Data

Heard, Christopher
    Dreaming aloud: the films of James Cameron

Includes index.

ISBN 0-385-25816-X

1. Cameron, James, 1954-   . 2. Motion pictures — United States.
3. Motion picture producers and directors — Canada — Biography.
I. Title

PN1998.3.C25H42 1998   791.43'0233'092   C98-931187-2

Front cover photo by Tibor Kolley/*The Globe and Mail*
Cover design by Kevin Connolly
Text design by Heidy Lawrance Associates
Printed and bound in Canada

Published in Canada by
Doubleday Canada Limited
105 Bond Street
Toronto, Ontario
M5B 1Y3

KRO   10 9 8 7 6 5 4 3 2 1

CONTENTS

For Debbie, who keeps me safe and warm

ACKNOWLEDGEMENTS

I would like to acknowledge the support, friendship, and hard work of my friend and editor Kathryn Exner at Doubleday Canada. Kathryn, without your encouragement and hard work, none of this would have been possible. Thanks also to the other fine folks at Doubleday Canada with whom I was lucky enough to be able to work: Christine Innes, Dara Rowland, Kristy Cook, Constance Mackenzie, and Gloria Goodman. Thanks also to Anne Holloway who helped me through the first wave.

Special thanks to Ben Rotterman who created *Reel to Real* and invited me to be a part of it. Without *Reel to Real*...who knows? Thanks also to my *Reel to Real* partner in madness, John H. Foote.

I would like to also thank David Gilmour. David, your guidance and advice was deeply appreciated and never steered me in any direction other than the right one.

Wild Bill Chambers, a movie mind as fast and expansive as a computer, thank you for your assistance.

My thanks to my family, my mother Marie Heard, my father Bill Heard, and my brother and friend Peter S. Heard.

Special thanks to Steve Johnson for all the interesting stories.

Also deserving of mention: Mandy Ketchinson, Kristie Sills, Lorraine Clark, Dan Duford, Christine Diakos, George

Kaufman, Julia Perry, Evan Soloman, Ethan Hawke for the congratulations, David Giammarco, the guys at Theatrebooks.

Extra special thanks to Heather MacGillivray and Natalie Amaral at Twentieth Century Fox. Heather and Natalie, your support and encouragement have meant more to me than I think you know.

And thanks to my pal Alfred Tonna. Alfred, you came through for me when I needed it, and your continued support means a lot to me. We should do a show together one day.

And finally, to Mary. Mary, I am sorry I missed you first time around. You are the sun in my universe.

"Some people say less is more. No. More is more and too much is never enough."

JAMES CAMERON

INTRODUCTION

The young James Cameron's rise in my independent film company was almost as meteoric as his dazzling subsequent career. From the beginning, he succeeded brilliantly in applying his unique combination of analytical, creative, and technological skills to filmmaking. It is difficult enough for a filmmaker to create the illusion of reality, but it is even tougher to create that same illusion in the genres of science fiction, fantasy and apocalyptic adventure — the genres in which James Cameron is a master. The convincing creation of new worlds, imaginary but plausible science, and the psychology and movement of the inhabitants of futuristic or unfamiliar worlds is perhaps the most challenging of all tasks that a filmmaker can undertake. James Cameron, with his genius in this area, can truly be described as a writer-director with a vision.

Cameron started as a model maker on the film *Battle Beyond the Stars*, written by John Sayles, which was the first movie to shoot at the studio I'd built in Venice. It was an ambitious project for us, a space action adventure taking place on various planets and involving the use of several disparate spaceships that had to be designed to reflect the nature and culture of characters from various societies, alien as well as human. Perhaps the first indication of James Cameron's talent was that he not only designed and executed these spaceship models with brilliance and economy, but also figured out how to shoot them so that they appeared to their best advantage in flight against a moving starry background. On seeing this work, I immediately promoted him to head up the special effects unit.

Next, he was promoted to art director, a position that, in a low-budget company shooting on extremely fast schedules, put even more demands on his visual creativity and practical resourcefulness. Once again, James Cameron came through with brilliance.

I remember the young James Cameron as a ferociously hard-working perfectionist who never hesitated to give 200 percent of his ideas, energy and talent to someone else's movie. For example, I recall walking onto the spaceship set of another science fiction movie we were making, on which Cameron was the art director, and noticing that the wall of the ship's main cabin looked bare. "Jim," I said, "get something to put up there — something to give it some visual field of interest, I don't care what it is." Jim jumped to immediately. I don't now remember exactly what he came up with, but I do know it looked good and it looked functional. (It may also have been from that time that the term "kluge" was coined at the studio as shorthand for stuff to make any expanse of wall, corridor, or other surface look more texturally interesting. The term is still in use at the studio today, but the technique was initiated by Jim Cameron.

There's no doubt in my mind that Jim always wanted to make his own movies, but he understood the essentially collaborative nature of the business. As a consequence, whatever job he was given to do he did supremely well. He graduated to second unit director, while still heading up the special effects department.

Jim's work as a second unit director immediately showed what a fine director he was going to be: in fact, his work was so precise and cut together so well that he was in demand to shoot more and more. He ended up storyboarding and shooting whole sequences rather than just the usual pick ups, inserts, and so on.

Jim Cameron's contributions to every movie he worked on at my company were brilliant, not simply because of their visual imagination and technical virtuosity but also, as is evidenced in his own movies, because of his understanding of story. James Cameron clearly has a strong sense of the power of myth and the emotional language of the unconscious as expressed in dreams — and nightmares. This awareness, combined with his skill in storytelling, both on the page and on the screen, distinguishes him as a filmmaker. His movies on first viewing always have a strikingly visceral impact, but they continue to haunt and intrigue us on successive viewings because of their underlying thematic richness and emotional depth.

Roger Corman

PREFACE

James Cameron is a young man. Given his boundless imagination and close relationship with his dreams, he will probably always be a young man. He is a filmmaker who has many more projects ahead of him and may redefine cinematic language a few more times before he is done.

My aim in writing *Dreaming Aloud* is to tell the story of an ordinary young man with extraordinary talent and drive who took Hollywood by storm. The films of James Cameron are fascinating studies in the transmogrification of storytelling and in wildly imaginative special visual effects. Cameron takes his own dreams and nightmares and uses them in his movies. Nothing is too big, too loud, or too spectacular. In other words, nothing is impossible.

My fascination with the life and works of James Cameron dates back to the summer of 1984, when Cameron indirectly inspired me. I was a twenty-one-year-old screenwriter who had just had his first screenplay optioned by a major Hollywood studio. I thought I was taking my first steps on the yellow brick road. The realities of Hollywood inevitably clashed with my youthful naiveté. It wasn't long before I had convinced myself that a Canadian kid from a small Ontario town faced insurmountable odds when rubbing up against the Hollywood dream factory.

One Sunday afternoon around this time I took in a matinee of James Cameron's breakout movie, *The Terminator*.

I knew little about the movie and my expectations were low. What I saw astounded me and resonated for years afterward. I was affected by the strange storyline, odd-looking actors, unforgettable and innovative special effects, and haunting music. After leaving the theater I was eager to find out all I could about the maker and the making of the movie. After doing some digging I found out that, like me, James Cameron was from a small town in Ontario. He had taken a script that nobody wanted to make and turned it into a blockbuster. Most important, he'd made it his way. He had cast an actor whom nobody wanted to cast and in the process turned Arnold Schwarzenegger into the highest-paid movie star on earth. With little money and little time he had made a movie that ended up on the *Time* magazine "Ten Best of the Year" list.

Ayrton Senna, the world-famous Formula One driver, used to describe himself this way: "I knew I had real greatness inside of me, I knew I was capable of truly great achievement — the task that I faced was going out and proving that to the world." I thought about James Cameron when I read those words. The films of James Cameron are fascinating in and of themselves but they become even more compelling when you look at what went into making each one of them. James Cameron proves every time out that, with talent, perseverance, and the stubborn refusal to accept no for an answer, anything can be done.

And it can be done even by someone from a small town in Ontario, Canada.

One

ONTARIO BORN, HOLLYWOOD BOUND

"Los Angeles ... Isn't that somewhere near Hollywood?"

JAMES CAMERON, AGE SEVENTEEN

Kapuskasing, Canada, has a population that hovers around eleven thousand souls and has for quite a while. There has always been a sense that Kapuskasing was in a state of flux. In 1913 this northwestern Ontario town became the site of an agricultural experiment in crop rotation that put it, if only in a small way, on the map. In 1914 Kapuskasing became a stop on the transcontinental railroad, and during the First World War it housed a huge prisoner-of-war camp. It looked as if boom times were about to dawn in 1922 when the Spruce Falls Power and Paper Plant was built to harness the raging power of the Smokey Falls and bring a stable industry and identity to the town. Although the plant provided employment it failed to attract the influx of industry that was anticipated.

James Cameron was born in Kapuskasing on August 16, 1954. His father, Phillip, worked as an electrical engineer in the paper mill. His mother, Shirley, was an artist and a homemaker. Phillip was a strict disciplinarian who unintentionally bequeathed to his son a healthy disrespect for authority. Shirley, on the other hand, encouraged young Jim to explore his artistic side and arranged for some of his paintings to be shown in a local gallery. His mother is the inspiration for a gravitation toward independent women that Jim Cameron has felt throughout his life; the women in Cameron's movies all have fiercely independent streaks. On the flip side, his father's strictness planted the seeds of an attraction to a career in which he can tell other people what to do and they actually listen. Cameron's sets are famous for being run with a military precision with General Cameron firmly in control of all aspects of making the movie.

Cameron became a tinkerer early in life. He and his younger brother, Mike, both loved to build and experiment, everything from go-carts and rafts to treehouses, almost as soon as their hands and his strength could do the bidding of his active imagination. One of young Jim's more spectacular inventions was a catapult that launched huge rocks through the air with sufficient height and velocity to dig craters where they landed. Another episode illustrates his insatiable hands-on curiosity about how things worked. This particular experiment cost the lives of several unfortunate mice when the submersible that Jim had designed and built sent them to their deaths over Niagara Falls.

Jim and Mike shared a close relationship that continues to this day. They were both somewhat nerdy characters who were often picked on. On one occasion, some neighborhood kids ripped off a few of Jim's toys. The brothers investigated the crime and determined that they knew with certainty who the culprits were. They decided not to get mad but to get even. Together they snuck into the offenders' yard and sawed through the branches that held their treehouse in place. When the dirty little crooks next climbed into their treehouse the entire structure toppled to the ground, sending at least one of them to the hospital.

The Camerons moved from Kapuskasing to Chippewa, near Niagara Falls, Ontario, in 1966, to follow Phillip Cameron's employment opportunities in hydro-electricity, and this is where young Jim began a journey that would eventually touch millions of people the world over.

Many people who have gone on to great achievement like to trace their evolution back to the one defining experience that molded them, when the map of the road ahead was first drawn. For young James Cameron that moment came when he was fifteen years old and went to his local theater to see *2001: A Space Odyssey*. He remembers the experience this way: "I just couldn't figure out how all those visual effects were done, and I wanted badly to know, to understand what I was seeing. I went back to see the movie ten times trying to get inside it."

Cameron quickly got his hands on any camera he could find. The second he obtained a beat-up old 16-mm camera he started messing around with models of spaceships and planets that he built himself, filming his own little intergalactic battles. This was truly a time of wonder for Cameron. He was dreaming wildly imaginative dreams, but he was also intensely interested in the mechanics behind fulfilling those dreams. "I remember lying awake in bed at night and listening to awful music while choreographing epic space battles in my head. I was imagining both the battle itself on a huge screen and ways to film it. This was frustrating given the lack of technical knowledge I had at that point."

Cameron was attending Stamford Collegiate at the time. He had a history teacher named Kathryn Englund whom he has often credited with having had a profound effect on him. To this day, most recently on the set of his record-smashing epic *Titanic*, when the subject of his high-school days comes up he mentions his beloved history teacher as someone who gave him the confidence to dream and dream big. In Nova Scotia in July of 1996 while making

Titanic, Cameron discovered that one of his crew members was not only from Niagara Falls but was also one of his fellow Stamford alumnae. Cameron asked the young woman if there was one teacher she especially remembered. Her answer: Ms. Englund. Cameron quickly and vividly described the effect that Ms. Englund had had on his life, then turned back to directing the most expensive epic in the history of moviemaking.

From early on, special effects were what interested Cameron the most about filmmaking. He continued to experiment with moviemaking in high school, but his inability to make realistic special effects frustrated him. His fascination for how images were created photographically was infinite, yet he could not see how he would ever be able to work in the movie business, living as he did so far away from where the bulk of films were made. He struggled with the notion that his interest in moviemaking might lead to nothing. Happily for Cameron, a neat twist of fate was about to nudge him toward his destiny.

One day in early 1971 Phillip Cameron came home from work to tell his family that he had been offered the opportunity to assume a better-paying position. The catch was that he would be required to relocate to Orange County, California. He then took each member of the family aside one by one to give particulars, answer questions, and gauge reactions. When it was Jim's turn, the teenager became excited when his father referred to the place they might move to as "Los Angeles." Jim thought about this for a moment, then asked, "Isn't that somewhere near Hollywood?" His father confirmed that Hollywood was indeed in Los Angeles County. Cameron expressed an immediate enthusiasm for the move, and it was decided that the Camerons would wait until the school year finished before packing up and moving to Southern California.

Instantly Cameron had realized that this move to California was his one shot to act on his dream of making movies, even though that was still a somewhat abstract goal. Once settled in Orange County, Cameron became disappointed and disillusioned when the realities of the movie world started to sink in. At least when he was living in Nowhereville, Ontario, he could use that as an excuse for delaying his dreams. But now he was in the crucible of filmmaking and not only had he no clue how to get his foot in the door — he didn't even know how to find the door. He was seventeen, just out of high school. In spite of his burning desire to attend film school, his family simply could not afford it.

Cameron eventually enrolled in Fullerton College to study physics, but he switched to English literature when he realized that he lacked the math skills to make it to the top. It was a confusing time for Cameron, who recalls, "I didn't know if I wanted to be a scientist or an artist. I know I had the temperament of an artist."

James Cameron is a perfectionist who always sets the

highest standards for himself. A salty self-revelation by comedian Redd Foxx also deftly describes Cameron. "I wanted to be the top guy in whatever I did," said Foxx. "That's why I quit being an altar boy at the church. Once I found out I'd never be Pope I said 'Fuck it!' " Cameron needs to believe that his efforts will take him to the highest echelons of achievement: if not the best on earth at whatever he's doing, at least one of the top stratum.

Scientists and filmmakers have much in common, says Cameron. They both must have the ability to think in the abstract if they are to produce important work. But a career as a physicist would not have quelled the other desire Cameron had, and that was the urge to be a storyteller, a dazzler through words and images. Perhaps if he had become a physicist he might well have written science fiction or fantasy novels on the side.

By 1976 Cameron was again stalled on the path to his dreams. He had dropped out of college; he had fallen head over heels in love with a local waitress named Sarah; they had married and moved into a small house. He made ends meet by driving a truck for the Orange County School District.

The summer of 1977 was a pivotal one in the history of movies, as it marked the release of George Lucas's *Star Wars*. Cameron went to the landmark movie and found that it spoke to him in a very personal way. "I was really upset when I saw *Star Wars*. That was the movie that I wanted to make. After seeing that movie I got very determined. I decided to get busy."

He haunted the University of Southern California library, reading everything he could get his hands on about movies, from scripts of his favorite films to dissertations on optical printing and front and rear projection effects. It was at this point that the way ahead became clear; his remembrance of this time is clear and unapologetic. "I seemed to be pulled toward visual effects. Cinema history wasn't of any great interest to me. I had no idea who Humphrey Bogart was."

Cameron began to buy lenses and other bits of cinematic apparatus and systematically take them apart to find out how they worked and how he might be able to alter them to achieve a different result. He built little sections of dolly tracks around his living room and started experimenting in any way his imagination and ingenuity prompted him. Today Cameron marvels at the turn his life was taking. He describes this period as a "complete transformation. I went from being a bum who liked to smoke dope and hang out by the river drinking beer and race around in a fast junk-heap car to this completely obsessed maniac. My wife at the time really thought I was crazy. Sarah was literally afraid of me."

This behavior at home was to set a trend. Cameron, while being a passionate man who loves women, becomes so completely absorbed in his work that any relationship he is in simply chokes to death from lack of oxygen.

Cameron methodically studied movies and the art of screenwriting. A good friend at the time was William Wisher, who would go on to co-write *Terminator 2: Judgment Day* with Cameron, and it was Wisher who really turned Jim on to the importance of the screenplay. Wisher had ambitions of being a screenwriter, and he would often drag Cameron along to haunt a bookstore in Hollywood that sold movie posters and other memorabilia, including photocopies of screenplays.

Even with his growing knowledge and boundless energy and enthusiasm, Cameron was still distant from real moviemaking. He had written several stories, including one that would eventually be developed into *The Abyss*, but they were all done in a straight narrative prose format. When he was introduced to screenplay format he gave it a stab but nothing came of it. Wisher got something of a break in 1979 when he was brought together with some dentists from nearby Tustin, California, who wanted to make a movie as a way of qualifying for a tax shelter. Wisher called Cameron to ask him if he had any ideas for a screenplay. They got together and formulated ten potential plots. *Star Wars* was still breaking box-office records, and one of the pair's ideas was a science fiction storyline. The other nine the two describe as "clichéd, bargain-basement, low-budget movie plots." This science fiction idea immediately grabbed the dentists, who hoped to capitalize on the phenomenal success of *Star Wars*. Cameron and his partner gave no thought at all to the fact that the scenario they had come up with involved some intricate space battles and exotic distant inhabited planets, things that cost money and required equipment to bring to life. Money and equipment they simply didn't have.

This was James Cameron's first taste of filmmaking. When he and Wisher sat down and wrote the proper screenplay, ideas came together with exciting and confidence-inspiring ease. So much so that just before they started work Cameron quit his truck driving job. On being told that he had to give two weeks' notice, he replied that he didn't have time. The moviemaking career of James Cameron began the next day.

Nothing ever came of that initial outing, but Cameron did finish the screenplay and still speaks of it fondly, even after his string of megahits. He knows that the script was all over the map with no structure, but the exercise did teach him something of the mechanics of moviemaking.

Emboldened, Cameron was ready to make some moves. His next step was to try to kick his way in through the door at the famed studio where so many brilliant filmmakers had first been allowed to flex their muscles. He decided to ask for a job at the company run by B-movie impresario Roger Corman, New World Pictures.

Two

IN THE ROGER CORMAN
FILM FACTORY

*"Roger Corman once said he could film the fall
of Rome with a dozen extras and a pickup truck.
I believe him."*

JAMES CAMERON

On April 5, 1926, Roger Corman, one of the most influential men in the history of motion pictures, was born in Detroit, Michigan. Corman's impact is far reaching: initially through New World Pictures and now through his Concorde/New Horizons Productions, he has assisted many of the most prolific filmmakers to enter the mainstream over the past twenty years. Francis Ford Coppola made his first movie with Corman. Martin Scorsese made his first movie with Corman. Jonathan Demme made his first movie with Corman. And the list goes on. Roger Corman started off making B-grade, drive-in-theater-type movies during the days of studio control and continued to make them after the B-movie was declared dead.

But discovering all this raw young talent was not the act of an altruistic philanthropist; rather, it was the work of the owner of a motion picture production company who wanted to make lots of movies for as little money as possible. To do this Corman was obliged to find the cheapest talent he could: young and panting for the opportunity to make movies. Corman got what he wanted, the young filmmakers got what they wanted. That is how Roger Corman became the undisputed king of the B-movie.

True to the Hollywood tradition, Corman entered the movie world by getting a job, in 1949, in the mailroom at Twentieth Century Fox, right out of a three-year hitch in the Navy. He had huge ambitions of becoming a filmmaker and was prepared to start at the bottom and work his way up. It was Corman's habit to comment on the scripts, books, and treatments he was asked to deliver to the various studio executives. Rather than being fired for poking his nose in where it didn't belong, he was promoted to story analyst for his insight and his eye for good material. After a few years of this Corman grew frustrated by the slowness in his rise to the top of the Hollywood heap. He quit his job in 1951 and left Hollywood altogether, landing in England, where he studied English literature at Oxford University.

But the lure of the movies remained something that Roger Corman could not shake, and after his British sojourn he realized that he needed to get back to Hollywood right away. He returned in 1952 and became a literary agent as a way to reconnect with the film industry. In 1953 Corman re-entered the movie business proper as a producer and screenwriter on a few instantly forgettable movies. In 1955 he made his debut as a director with the undistinguished *Five Guns West* and quickly followed that with the equally forgettable *Apache Woman*.

Corman tried to tap into current fads by making teenage hot rod movies, westerns, gangster movies, and science fiction movies when they were in vogue. His output was unbelievable. In 1957 alone he made ten movies, some that were shot in as few as three days. It was when Corman started making gothic horror movies that he struck a chord. In 1964 he made two movies in England based on literary works of Edgar Allan Poe. *The Masque of the Red Death* and *The Tomb of Ligeia* were slickly produced, sufficiently well acted, and scary enough to attract audiences then and develop a cult following that remains loyal today.

Most of Corman's movies, a staggering seventy-five in fifteen years, were made mainly for another low-budget legend, Sam Arkoff, and his American International Pictures. In 1970 Corman decided to dive in with both feet and form his own company. New World Pictures was formed with his brother Gene.

It was during the 1970s that Corman began producing movies rather than directing them. He used his clout to branch out into distribution, bringing Ingmar Bergman's *Cries and Whispers* and Federico Fellini's *Amarcord* to North American audiences.

Today Corman's most recent movies have become sadly derivative of current movie tastes and trends. When *Jurassic Park* was chewing up box-office records, Corman answered with his own version, called *Carnosaur*. While the *Jurassic Park* sequel, *The Lost World*, was being planned and negotiated, Corman pumped out *Carnosaur 2*. By the time *The Lost World* made it into theaters, Corman's *Carnosaur 3* was already in video stores. People may like to treat themselves to expensive restaurants every now and then, but Corman knows that they will still line up at Burger King.

In 1983 Corman sold his New World Pictures for $17 million to a group of investors who were interested in the catalog of movies owned by the company. He quickly set up another company, Millennium, to continue functioning as a producer. A year later he founded another production company, New Horizons, and a distribution company, Concorde Pictures. He continues to oversee the production and distribution of low-budget movies. In 1990 he wrote his autobiography, *How I Made a Hundred Movies in Hollywood and Never Lost a Dime.*

James Cameron entered the Roger Corman movie factory in 1979, at a time when the glut of enormously gifted young filmmakers seemed to be drying up and the big studios were scooping talented young moviemakers directly out of film school. Corman was in a spell of making movies that were on the ambitious side, in response to the popularity of the *Star Wars* wave of effects-heavy science fiction movies. His budgets were heading past $1 million and sometimes even topping $2 million. (In 1990 Corman would step behind the camera for the first time in twenty years when he made the interesting *Frankenstein Unbound* for a whopping $18 million.) For James Cameron, Corman's studio could not have been more fertile. He was a science fiction fanatic who had a real talent for illustration and design. Armed with a clutch of spaceship models, he went to New World Pictures hoping to land a job.

He applied for the job of special effects cameraman, but New World had all the cameramen they wanted. New World was about to go into production on a space epic called *Battle Beyond the Stars* and they were in need of a miniature-model builder. Cameron didn't want to start that far down the crew list, but he recognized the job as an opportunity he could exploit.

Once hired he quickly moved up. For some reason, the

design of the hero's spaceship had been overlooked. No one could come up with an interesting enough concept for it until Cameron thrust his best foot forward and said, "I can do that." This initiative put him face to face with the legendary Roger Corman himself. Corman was interested in meeting all his designers and overseeing all the designs. He is known for his egalitarianism. It doesn't matter who you are on the crew list, if you have ideas he wants to hear them; if they are workable and creative they will be used and you will be rewarded. As a result of this meeting with Corman, Cameron was handed the task of creating the hero's ship, which gave him the opportunity to insinuate himself into other aspects of the movie's production.

Cameron had little practical knowledge of filmmaking, but he didn't let this lack stand in the way of approaching Corman with an idea for a bold new production technique.

During the production of *Battle Beyond the Stars,* a miniature unit was working in one area of the studio while a live-action unit filmed lead actors George Peppard and Robert Vaughn in another part of the studio. The problem this system presented was that the live-action stuff looked very different from what was being done in miniature, and the technology wasn't available — at least at the New World budget level — to blend the work of the two units convincingly.

Cameron pitched Corman on the idea of getting some matte paintings done. Matte paintings are large paintings that are photographed separately and composited with other elements. They provide background scenery or extensions of a set, such as putting an outer space background behind a model spaceship. Once the matte paintings were done, Cameron suggested some process photography that would seamlessly blend the work of the two units into a cohesive picture that would look much more realistic. Process shots are shots taken against a moving or still background consisting of previously filmed footage that is projected through a transparent screen behind the action being filmed.

Cameron told Corman he could easily do what he proposed, even though he had never attempted either technique on this level before. What Cameron was saying was that such techniques could be done and he should be the one to do them. Corman liked the idea of increasing production values without spending a lot of money or wasting a lot of time. Overnight James Cameron became the head of a newly created visual effects department. He took over a small office, made a plate with his name on it, and taped it to the door. Knowing that he now must come up with the goods, he seized the challenge with characteristic vigor, ending up inventing a rudimentary improvised front-screen projection system that is still in use.

What made New World Pictures an interesting place to work was that no one there was an expert on anything. Everyone made his or her own contribution based on instinct, imagination, and self-taught technical know-how.

Among Cameron's colleagues at New World Pictures were the Skotak brothers, Robert and Dennis, who would go on to win an Academy Award for their visual effects work on James Cameron's *Aliens*. Again Corman found himself on the cutting edge almost by accident. He was not developing a lot of writers and directors at this time, but he was shepherding a generation of talents who would go on to develop techniques that would revolutionize special visual effects in some of the most spectacularly successful movies in history.

Cameron asserted his newfound authority by firing the art director on *Battle Beyond the Stars*, replacing him with himself, and combining the art department with the visual effects department. He managed this maneuver by convincing Corman that even more money and time could be saved.

At this time they had ahead of them the designs of twenty-two spacecraft interior sets and planetary surface sets. Production was about to begin and they barely had two sets built. This was not uncommon on New World Pictures sets, where fast and cheap was the rule. This new visual effects/art department worked in three shifts, a day shift, a swing shift, and a night shift — James Cameron himself worked all three shifts.

Battle Beyond the Stars (1980) was an interesting little science fiction movie that is still something of a curiosity today. The storyline is patterned after Akira Kurosawa's *Seven Samurai*. A group of heroic characters is brought together to defend a peaceful planet of colonists against an armada of evil characters bent on taking over the planet for their own use.

Cameron's art direction is not spectacular but is impressive, given that this was the first commercial movie he had ever worked on. Cameron, director Jimmy Murakami, and the rest of the crew were working with a minuscule budget. When *Battle Beyond the Stars* was sold to television in 1982, network executives worried about the extent to which actress Sybil Danning's rather prominent breasts were revealed. A computerized coverup of her décolletage was undertaken, and the budget for this digital operation exceeded the budget that James Cameron had had to execute his entire complement of special visual effects.

Viewers who read the small-print credits at the end of *Battle Beyond the Stars* will see an important name flash by. The production manager is Gale Anne Hurd, a future partner, both professionally and personally, of James Cameron.

Hurd graduated with honors from Stanford University and went directly from that achievement to joining New World Pictures in 1977 as Corman's executive assistant. But she had loftier ambitions that she was confident she would be able to fulfill under Corman. Like everyone at New World Pictures, she pitched in and lent her labor and her ideas whenever they were needed. Soon she was doing a lot more than answering Mr. Corman's telephone. Just four years after walking in the New World Pictures front door, she was allowed to co-produce *Smokey Bites the Dust*. Hurd and Cameron met at New World Pictures and worked together on a couple of projects, but it wasn't until they both left the Roger Corman nest that they would change the face of moviemaking together.

That first experience with producing ignited a passion in Hurd to which she was ready to give full rein with one film under her belt. She left New World Pictures in 1982 and formed her own production company, Pacific Western Productions.

James Cameron was so blindly ambitious that he quickly rose through the ranks at New World Pictures, sometimes leapfrogging over several job titles and landing on his feet in yet another position for which he had few qualifications. Cameron's tunnel vision didn't keep him from recognizing that he was becoming unpopular with others in the company. Today he admits, "Everybody else who worked there really hated me, and I don't blame them."

Cameron was active on several movies for a day here and a day there, an idea here and an idea there. In 1980 he was asked to work on John Carpenter's *Escape from New York*, a movie that was successful enough to inspire a sequel sixteen years later. Carpenter had a limited budget but he wanted some impressive visual effects, and he wanted the guy who made *Battle Beyond the Stars* look so dynamic for next to nothing.

John Carpenter had been a young film student with a

fascination for the work of Howard Hawks and John Ford. He made a promising little movie called *Assault on Precinct 13* in 1975, which he described as his version of his beloved westerns, about a police precinct about to be decommissioned that is attacked by a street gang. From there he teamed up with his writing and producing partner Debra Hill to make a horror film that would go on to become one of the most successful independent movies ever made. Carpenter made the landmark *Halloween* on a budget of slightly less than $400,000. It has made back an estimated $100 million since its release in 1978.

Escape from New York is set in the year 1997 in a United States that has started to win the war on crime by forming a national police force, sealing off Manhattan Island and turning it into one huge maximum-security prison. The president's plane crashes in Manhattan, and a war hero from a war between the United States and Russia in the mid-1990s, who has been sentenced to life in prison for armed robbery and murder, is called in to rescue the chief executive.

Carpenter was planning a scene that had hero Snake Plissken (Kurt Russell) flying a glider into the core of Manhattan and landing atop the World Trade Center. He was shooting in St. Louis, Missouri, which was problem number one. He also wanted shots of a computerized three-dimensional grid map on the control panel of the glider so he could switch to a full-screen shot, allowing the audience to "fly" through this computerized representation of downtown Manhattan. Problem number two was that the technology did not exist to shoot such a scene and graft it successfully into the movie.

James Cameron's solution was a stroke of pure genius. He built a miniature cardboard model of a cross-section of the Manhattan core and painted it black. He then painstakingly outlined each building in Day-Glo paint. He set up his camera and moved it slowly through the model skyscrapers. The result is a perfect-looking computer screen version of what a Manhattan block would look like on a computerized grid map. Even on careful repeat viewings it is impossible to tell that you are not watching a computerized 3-D grid map. When asked to describe how he remembered his first viewing of the footage, Carpenter replies, "Jim Cameron's work just knocked me on my ass. I assigned him something I knew was impossible to do and he did it with a brilliant simplicity and dedication to achievement."

Cameron's next film for New World Pictures was another science fiction thriller, *Galaxy of Terror,* in 1981. The skimpy storyline concerns a group of people on a spaceship who respond to an SOS beacon and end up on a planet where whatever horror they have deep in their subconscious turns into a real and terrifying situation. Everything about this movie harkens back to Ridley Scott's groundbreaking gothic horror in space, *Alien,* released to much acclaim two summers earlier — everything from the isolated setting to a blatant, almost cut-for-cut re-creation of the famous scene from *Alien* in which a life form incubating in one of the crew members (John Hurt) makes a sensational entrance by exploding through his chest. Again Cameron's duties were multifaceted: he is credited as the production designer but he also functioned as second unit director and creator of special effects, including one of a gruesome severed arm that is covered with writhing maggots.

Cameron worked only a few weeks on *Galaxy of Terror* when destiny intervened. Roger Corman was describing to a group of people, James Cameron among them, the complexity of directing a motion picture when the following exchange took place:

Corman: Anyone who can operate a turret lathe can direct a motion picture.

Cameron: I can operate a turret lathe. I used to work as a machinist.

Corman: I'll think about it.

Cameron's time at New World Pictures was about to come to an end, but the lessons he learned during his stay there were to endure throughout his career.

Three

"THE BEST FLYING PIRANHA MOVIE EVER MADE"

"Even though it was his first movie Jim was pretty much the way he is now ... He was completely obsessed with his work."

ACTOR LANCE HENRIKSEN

From the opening credit sequence of *Piranha 2: The Spawning*, with its look and tone that are reminiscent of films by spaghetti western director Sergio Leone, audiences suspect they are in store for a low-budget horror movie. *Very* low budget. Suspicions are quickly confirmed by the first few scenes. The film opens with some interestingly shot underwater footage of a man and woman diving in crystal-blue Caribbean waters. They are exploring a sunken ship that has become a habitat for tropical fish. Once in the wreck, the female diver removes her bathing suit and proceeds to seduce her diving partner. She takes out his knife and cuts his bathing suit off him. Overcome by passion and foolhardiness, they abandon their scuba breathing apparatus before making love under water. While they are in the midst of this aquatic sexual activity, they are attacked and ripped to pieces by noisy little creatures the audience doesn't see. Cut to a tropical beach, where a teenaged boy named Chris is strolling with fishing gear in hand. Cut to a long, tanned female leg that Cameron's camera lovingly traverses. It belongs to Anne, the manager of a tourist resort on this unnamed Caribbean island, and the mother of Chris. The son approaches his naked mother, who is only barely covered by a thin white sheet, and puts a gulping tropical fish in front of her. She has obviously seen too many of these ugly fish to react strongly to them. The pair then engage in a giggling wrestling match on the mother's bed that makes the audience uncomfortable with its hint at incestuous goings-on.

The rest of *Piranha 2* is either completely predictable or bewilderingly uninvolving. A government experiment has gone horribly wrong, producing a mutated species of piranha that can fly and is exceedingly vicious. At the resort plans are being made for a giant party that involves all the guests being on the beach to watch the annual spectacle of silvery grunions spawning in the shallow water. There is a lawman on the island, played by gravelly voiced Lance Henriksen in one of his first lead roles, who must try to figure out what these killer fish are and try to save the day.

All in all *Piranha 2: The Spawning* is a lackluster movie that would be completely forgotten were it not for the fact that it can be looked back on as the film in which James Cameron made his directorial debut. The performances are amateurish, with the exception of Henriksen, who seems to be the only person in the cast who is attempting to act in spite of the script. The effects are low rent and the story is so full of holes that it looks as if a school of piranhas has chewed through it. The underwater footage is arresting, and if there is anything in *Piranha 2* that gives an indication of what was to come from James Cameron it is these scuba diving sequences. But even they can't raise this movie above the level of forgettable.

Corman has distribution connections all over the world, and one of these, Italian producer Ovidio G. Assonitis, was about to start production on a quickie sequel to Joe Dante's quirky little horror movie *Piranha* — made in 1978 from a cleverly written screenplay by John Sayles (*Lone Star*) — and he was having trouble with the director he had originally chosen. Corman had an international distribution deal with Warner Bros., so he and Assonitis got together. Their first priority was to hire a new director. They wanted a first-timer for two reasons: to save money and to make sure they had someone who was grateful enough for the job to take orders from the very hands-on Assonitis without question. Corman immediately thought of James Cameron.

Cameron was still working on *Galaxy of Terror* for Corman when he was plucked from the set and hired as the director of *Piranha 2*. Cameron was delighted and, in spite of the obvious low-rent aspect of the picture, he was determined to do everything he could to make this the best possible movie he could for the money he had. Cameron agreed to do the movie without even seeing the script. He asked only to be assured that he was going to be making a semi-mainstream movie and not a porno flick. Once he was given that assurance he was keen to start. The first day of principal photography on the Jamaican location was only three weeks away.

Cameron had done many jobs for Corman and New World Pictures but one role he hadn't taken on was screen-writer. The only screenwriting he had done was the aborted movie project for the dentists from Tustin. No matter, he read the *Piranha 2* screenplay, written by H. A. Milton, and felt that it needed a quick polish. He wanted to make it better but he also wanted to make it his own. He tried hard to push the script toward being more atmospheric, character driven, and suspenseful, but he quickly came to realize that when you are making a movie about an attack of flying piranha fish there is only so much punching up you can do.

When James Cameron arrived in Jamaica in February 1981 eager to start directing his first motion picture, his spirits quickly crashed. He found that the badly organized crew spoke mainly Italian and that the production was woefully underfinanced. When his assigned special effects crew brought him the rubber piranhas that were needed for the movie, he was so disappointed that he stayed up nights making his own flying fish and painting them by hand. When it came time to use the flying piranhas in scenes, the results were unintentionally hilarious. In one sequence, where two scantily clad party girls go out on the water for a midnight boat ride that includes drinking and nude swimming, a group of flying piranhas attack. The effect was achieved by filling a bushel basket with rubber piranhas and tossing them in front of the camera.

Lance Henriksen, who has since worked on two higher-profile James Cameron films (*The Terminator* and *Aliens*) and become a close friend of Cameron's, was impressed by his first brush with the novice director. He had never before seen such fierce dedication to a task that few would feel deserved such a focused, determined effort. He recalls his first encounter with Cameron: "I remember thinking to myself, 'Who is this guy?' Even though it was his first movie Jim was pretty much the way he is now. He took a nothing script and he tried to make it something. He would survive on three hours of sleep a night. He was completely obsessed with his work."

Cameron was constantly at odds with Ovidio Assonitis, who would take the shot footage, process it, then refuse to show Cameron or any other member of the crew the dailies. He would often berate Cameron, telling him that the footage was garbage and that it simply would not cut together. Cameron told Assonitis that he needed to see the footage before he could understand what needed to be done or not done. Assonitis and his front men were so disruptive that, fifteen minutes before the cameras were to roll, they would show up on the set armed with pages of new script that included long monologues they insisted be shot with no changes at all.

Cameron's growing friendship with Lance Henriksen provided some comfort; at least he had one ally. Henriksen had worked with Assonitis before on the low-budget *The Visitor* (1979). Assonitis had shown *The Visitor* to Cameron and suggested that the American actor with the malevolent voice who had appeared in small roles in *Dog Day Afternoon* and *Close Encounters of the Third Kind* be cast in *Piranha 2: The Spawning*. There were no stuntmen on *Piranha 2*, so all the actors were asked to do their own stunts. Henriksen did one stunt that involved jumping out of a helicopter flying about forty feet above the water. The scene showed the lawman plunging into the water to save his son and his girlfriend, who are stranded in a rowboat in piranha-infested waters. What makes this scene completely idiotic is the fact that Henriksen is the only one in the helicopter; the vacated helicopter crashes into the sea. Henriksen broke his hand in the fall and finished the movie in great pain.

Cameron managed to struggle through the long days and nights of shooting enduring one frustration after another. When the costumes were unsuitable Cameron had his cast improvise by wearing their own clothing. Lance Henriksen bought the shirt off the back of a local waiter because it looked more like a shirt that a law officer would wear than the one he was given by the costume designer.

Once shooting was completed, Cameron's problems began in earnest. He was still not being shown any of his footage and was not a part of the editing process. Assonitis had decided that he knew better how to make this movie playable and that, as far as he was concerned, Cameron's services were no longer needed. So enraged was Cameron by this exclusion that he took drastic action. From Jamaica he flew to Rome to confront Assonitis at his office. Cameron's anger must have been terrifyingly apparent, because throughout the entire confrontation Assonitis sat behind his desk with a letter opener poised for action, as if he was afraid that Cameron was going to fly over the desk at him at any minute.

Cameron was incensed that his name was going to appear on a movie that he had had no say in. He decided to take matters firmly into own hands. One night he snuck into the editing facilities and slipped the lock on the editing room with a credit card. Once inside he was surrounded by film cans. With great determination he sorted through the cans, but they were all labeled in Italian. He found one that had *fine* written on it. Knowing that meant end in Italian, he figured he would start there and work his way backward. Night after night Cameron snuck in and recut footage until he had recut the entire movie into a version that he thought was still terrible but that he could call his own. He was eventually caught and threatened with criminal charges, but the charges were never pressed. The movie was again recut by Assonitis and his crew and, a full two years after its completion, was released in their version. In some markets *Piranha 2: The Spawning* was released as *Piranha 2: Flying Killers*, but it's the same version.

Throughout this escapade, Cameron was living in a Rome hotel, flat broke — so broke that he would search the hallways for room service trays left for pickup, grabbing any half-eaten food he could find. He was also suffering from depression and a bad case of the flu that laid him out in his hotel room for several feverish days and nights. During this bout of sickness, Cameron was struck by inspiration in the form of a hallucinatory dream. Its most striking image was of a metal skeleton dragging itself across the floor using kitchen knives. Cameron woke from this dream and started making notes.

Every major director has a *Piranha 2: The Spawning* in their filmography. Oliver Stone made his directorial debut with a low-budget Canadian horror movie, *Seizure*, made in Montreal in 1974. George Lucas made a chilling little science fiction movie, *THX 1138*, in 1971. Martin Scorsese directed something called *Boxcar Bertha* in 1972 for Roger Corman, and Francis Coppola made an obscure film in Ireland called *Dementia 13* (1963), also for Roger Corman. To his credit Cameron does not try to make excuses for *Piranha 2*; he proudly if ironically calls it "the best flying piranha movie ever made." *Variety* said about the movie, "Special effects experts come up with convincing enough gore but the monsters are laughably phony. This is a routine monster film with an idiotic premise." No matter how awful this movie is, and it certainly is terrible by any standards, *Piranha 2: The Spawning* did play a pivotal role in the development of James Cameron, filmmaker. He finished it. It gave him a sense of accomplishment. It gave him his first directorial credit and an insight into the many challenges the helmsman on a movie must face. Most of all it gave him the confidence to forge ahead with the knowledge that he could pull it off no matter how difficult the circumstances. Since *Piranha 2* Cameron has faced adversity in project after project, but his directorial temperament thrives on almost insuperable challenges.

Four

CAMERON VS.
RAMBO

*"I hate writing. It is the most tedious, solitary,
terrifying part of the making of the film."*
JAMES CAMERON

The screenplay that was born that feverish night in Rome
was *The Terminator*. This screenplay marked the first real
success Cameron had as a writer. He wrote it entirely on
spec, meaning that he wrote it for himself without being
commissioned, as a sample work for his agent to show
around to the studios as an audition piece. This screenplay
was sufficiently impressive to net Cameron two opportunities that would solidify his ascension to Hollywood's A-list.

In 1981 *The Terminator* screenplay was sold to Hemdale Pictures, but it would be a full two and a half years before the cameras would roll. In the meantime Cameron received two script assignments, both sequels to successful movies, on the same day. His good fortune was almost unimaginable, and he didn't know which of the two to accept — so he took them both. One was to write a screenplay called *The Mission*, the title of which was later changed to *Rambo: First Blood Part II*. He also signed on to write *Alien 2*, which he later renamed *Aliens*.

Both sequels were follow-ups to movies that were considered mold breakers. Ridley Scott's 1979 summer release *Alien* was an eerie, gothic outer space horror movie that broke many of the visual conventions of its science fiction genre. Until *Alien*, movie spaceships were usually gleaming, antiseptic vehicles staffed by crews dressed in spiffy, perfectly fitting uniforms. Ridley Scott and writer Dan O'Bannon made their spaceship, the *Nostromo*, a filthy, grimy hulk staffed by a band of misfits in ill-fitting clothes. Scott enlisted the talents of Swiss artist H. R. Giger to give the movie a look unlike anything movie audiences had seen before. The alien landscapes and creatures were given a creepy biomechanical appearance that was the stuff of nightmares.

Likewise *First Blood*, released in 1982, the movie that introduced audiences to the character of John Rambo, took the returning Vietnam War veteran and built an action movie not around revenge but around self-defense and self-analysis. The movie was based on David Morrell's interesting novel of the same title and gave Sylvester Stallone his first hit outside of the *Rocky* series. After the first *Rocky* film in 1976 Stallone had tried the period drama *F.I.S.T.* with director Norman Jewison. He played a character fashioned after vanished Teamster boss Jimmy Hoffa, and audiences just didn't buy it. Stallone then wrote, directed, starred in, and composed and sang the title song for a movie based on his own first attempt at novel writing, *Paradise Alley* (1978), and again audiences stayed away in droves. Stallone was in the throes of a major case of believing his own press clippings. He wouldn't see major success again until he stepped back in the ring as Rocky Balboa for *Rocky II* in 1979.

Canadian director Ted Kotcheff, maker of *The Apprenticeship of Duddy Kravitz*, based on Mordecai Richler's classic coming-of-age novel, talked Stallone into making *First Blood*, but Stallone insisted on being allowed to rewrite the screenplay as a condition to his signing on. Kotcheff and Stallone worked on the screenplay and found that it came together quickly.

Kirk Douglas was cast opposite Stallone as his wartime mentor, Colonel Trautman. After filming began, though, Douglas dropped out amidst some controversy. The older star and Stallone were not getting along and Douglas was disturbed by the level of violence that was creeping into

rewritten drafts of the screenplay. He was replaced by veteran character actor Richard Crenna. Stallone was badly
injured in a fall from a tree during a dangerous stunt that
he insisted on performing himself. And the arsenal of
weapons kept on the set for the action sequences was stolen,
only to be partially recovered four months later in Belfast
during a raid on an I.R.A. hideout. But when all was said
and done, the, movie was successful and controversial
because of its politics, and popular because of its action,
stylish direction, and the stoic performance by Stallone.

When Cameron tackled John Rambo, he paid more
attention to the dramatic and psychological aspects of the
character. He can write action with the best of them but
he felt strongly that the character had huge dramatic potential. He saw John Rambo as a man betrayed by his country who remained loyal to it only to be betrayed yet again.

Cameron's *Rambo* screenplay was accepted as a perfect
blueprint for an action-packed new direction in which to
take the character. But Sylvester Stallone, as he does on all
his movies, rewrote the screenplay to fit his own sensibilities and, more important, his acknowledged limitations.
Cameron was less than happy with the results. Stallone had
retained the style and most of the situations and had left the
action sequences pretty much the same, but he had taken
out a lot of the character's depth and the philosophical
dimension of the story.

The James Cameron screenplay had a different way of

dealing with the prisoners-of-war that John Rambo was returning to the jungles of Vietnam to rescue. Cameron wrote these POWs as real people whose stories were interspersed throughout the screenplay. In the finished movie, the POWs are little more than symbols for the larger issue of American soldiers supposedly still being held as POWs in Vietnam and their country's seeming indifference to their plight. Cameron went to the trouble of researching this issue so he could give this action movie an air of authenticity that most action movies lack.

Cameron readily admits that his screenplay was unwieldy and overly ambitious, but he maintains that sometimes fewer explosions and more lines of dialogue are the solution to a dramatic problem. Without any dramatic substance the POWs provide little motivation for Rambo's heroism. "It was almost like they were parachuting into 'Nam to pick up a six-pack of beer," says Cameron. He acknowledges that he played no part in the production of *Rambo* and was not privy to decisions about the budget and schedule.

Perhaps the biggest change of all made in Cameron's *Rambo* was the removal of the "buddy" concept from the screenplay. At the suggestion of producer Buzz Feitshans, Cameron's screenplay contained another lead character who was to be at Stallone's side throughout as a sidekick, sounding board, and voice of reason. Cameron wrote four complete drafts of the screenplay, all of them containing this sidekick character. As interesting as these scripts were,

Stallone sounded an alarm. Cameron had given all the good lines to the sidekick. This was not to slight Stallone, says Cameron, but rather to accentuate Rambo's silent stoicism. When Stallone assumed the writing chores the first thing to go was the sidekick, even though there was talk that John Travolta would be offered the role.

(In a strange turn of events, the author of the novel, David Morrell, was hired to novelize the *Rambo* screenplay for a mass-market paperback. Morrell liked where Cameron was going with his original characters and concepts, and he used Cameron's drafts as well as what Stallone wrote as the basis for his novelization. Many of the witty lines of dialogue written for the sidekick that were excised from the movie found their way back into the novelization, even though the sidekick character himself was not written in.)

Cameron went to see *Rambo: First Blood Part II* after it opened and felt oddly detached throughout. He had had nothing to do with this movie other than his screenplay contribution, but he did allow himself a few moments of pride when the audience responded to what was left of his script in exactly the way that he had hoped they would, even though what he had written had been reinterpreted a few times along the way. This proved a theory that Cameron has that if it works on the page, it will work on the screen — no matter how many times it is stepped on.

The released version of *Rambo: First Blood Part II* turned an interesting idea into a comic-book refighting of the

Vietnam War with a few jingoistic lines of dialogue thrown in by Stallone to add his version of depth. In this revisionist view of the Vietnam War the good guys were allowed to win. John Rambo was reduced from a three-dimensional human being to a killing machine who could not be killed no matter who shot at him or tortured him how many times. Stallone showed off his newly sculpted body as often as he could and brandished a heavy, hard-to-fire M-60 machine gun with one hand.

Rambo: First Blood Part II was enormously successful and set box-office records in the summer of 1985, when it was released. It also set a dangerous summertime movie precedent: if you keep the dialogue and characterization to a bare minimum and the explosions and gunfire coming with regularity, then you have a decent chance of having a $100-million hit on your hands. *Variety* called the movie "one mounting fireball" and it is looked upon with disdain by most critics. Pauline Kael accurately described the movie this way in *The New Yorker:* "What Sylvester Stallone chooses to call a movie is a wired-up version of the narcissistic jingoism of the John Wayne–Second World War pictures. Its comic-strip patriotism exploits the pent-up rage of the Vietnam vets who feel that their country mistreated them after the war, and it preys on the suffering of the families who don't know what happened to their missing-in-action sons or brothers, fathers or husbands. A Sylvester Stallone hit movie has the same basic appeal as professional wrestling or demolition derbies: audiences hoot at it and get a little charged up at the same time."

Oddly enough, James Cameron considers screenwriting the weakest aspect of what he does. He enjoys the result, the screenplay that he considers the blueprint of the film, but he says he despises writing. "It is the most tedious, solitary, terrifying part of the making of the film. It is the moment when the creative die is cast, although it will take months and maybe years, and millions of dollars, to find out if the throw was a lucky one or not." And getting started is the first hurdle. "The blank page — I'll circle around that sucker for weeks," he admits.

Cameron describes the first day of writing a screenplay as "terrifying." By the time he finally gets down to it he has already cleaned his house to within an inch of its life and has arranged all the books on the shelves in alphabetical order by author.

Cameron starts the writing process by sitting in a comfortable easy chair and thinking. Just thinking and drinking lots of coffee. He ponders the story elements he will be dealing with until they start to take some shape. He juggles all the various elements until they fall into some kind of order, then he bangs out a quick outline that strings together the main visual and dramatic set pieces. Onto this he grafts a bare-bones storyline. Cameron likes to present a big visual set piece around the middle of the second act and bring together the various dramatic threads in the third act.

Some writers make copious research notes. Some write their scene ideas on index cards and rearrange them until convinced they are in the proper order before drafting the screenplay. This is a preferred technique of famed screen-writer Robert Towne, who wrote *Chinatown* and, most recently, his version of *Mission: Impossible*. Cameron prefers to think through his entire storyline first. Once he embarks on the actual writing he does all his work at night, often working from 6 p.m. to 7 a.m., when he packs it in and retires to bed. During the day he conducts his other busi-ness, with a hectic schedule of phone calls and meetings. He cannot write with any of these distractions happening. He drives himself almost around the clock like this for three or four weeks until the screenplay is finished. He enforces a strict self-discipline and commits himself to fin-ishing the screenplay as quickly as possible. At times he works himself into such a frenzy that he writes straight through until the end once the end is in sight. The last thirty pages of *Terminator 2: Judgment Day* were written in one thirty-two-hour-straight writing session.

Cameron took this modus operandi to the furthest reaches of sanity when he was writing *Rambo: First Blood Part II* and *Aliens*. He was committed to writing both screenplays at once; as well, he had a definite start date for production on *The Terminator* only months away rushing at him like a speeding train. "So I sat down and I said, 'Okay, I've got X number of days, that translates into X number of working hours.' I figured out exactly how many hours it takes me to write an average page and divided that into the time that I had. The mathematics worked on paper. But I simply had to meet that target, so it was X number of pages per day and per week. By being that methodical I could always tell if I was ahead or behind."

Cameron can write this way because he always starts from a fairly detailed treatment. These treatments are usually fifty or sixty pages long, single spaced, and they describe virtually every scene in the movie in prose style. An illustration of his method can be seen in the version of his *Strange Days* (1995) screenplay published by Penguin Books. The result is a revealing blend of dialogue, character sketches, and prose-style action sequences. What makes this work interesting is its unfinished feel. The reader gets the distinct impression of reading a work in progress, and is allowed a glimpse into the process of Cameron's screenwriting. It has been only recently that screenplays have been given any respect as literary creations; a published work in gestation like Cameron's *Strange Days* book is unprecedented.

By using such an extensive treatment, Cameron ends up with screenplays that run to about 150 pages. One page of a standard screenplay usually translates to one minute of screen time, so these first drafts must then be tightly edited. All of the fat is stripped away until only the meat of the story remains. Sometimes editing still can't bring the movie down to the length most studios feel comfortable with. In the case of *Aliens,* Cameron's screenplay translated into a movie that would have had a running time of about 180 minutes. Twentieth Century Fox said that this was simply far too long for a summertime release. Cameron agonized over the editing and cut it down to 137 minutes, and he had to defend his still lengthy running time to the studio. He successfully argued that the hugely successful third film in the *Star Wars* trilogy, *Return of the Jedi,* was exactly the same length and had returned well over $100 million at the box office. The problem with the *Aliens* screenplay was that Cameron had painted himself dramatically into a corner. There was no further cutting he could do without having the story suffer. He firmly believes that all the production values and spectacular visuals in the world are meaningless without a solid story.

James Cameron is a self-taught writer who has learned his craft through experience and generally makes his own rules. He subscribes to the belief that film is a limiting medium, that reaction shots are reaction shots no matter how well trained or experienced an actor is. A screenplay is meant to be seen, not read.

He is a big believer in a strong third act, citing something he calls the "recentcy effect," meaning that an audience is most affected by whatever they have seen most recently. *Aliens* is a classic example of his philosophy in action. The character of Hudson, played with a frenetic energy by Cameron mainstay Bill Paxton, is constantly on the screen throughout the first two-thirds of the movie, and has been given terrific lines. The final third of the movie focuses on Ripley (Sigourney Weaver) and her struggles. When the audience left the theater and when journalists sat down to write about *Aliens* it was Sigourney Weaver they talked about. They remembered her, Cameron says, because she was the last person they saw.

Though Cameron alleges that for him screenwriting is little more than a means to an end, a transitional phase between what is in his head and what ends up on the screen, his films remain remarkably true both in action and dialogue to his screenplays. This is rare in an era of multiple drafts and numerous writers for each film. Few directors shoot exactly what is in the original script any more. A recent highly publicized example of this trend is *The Devil's Own* (1997), in which a script by Kevin Jarre that was accepted by the movie's two stars, Harrison Ford and Brad Pitt, ended up being rewritten and rewritten until the movie scarcely resembled the original idea that put the project in motion. David Cronenberg is another director/writer who writes tight, economical scripts and then shoots them as they are written. Still, says Cameron, "I do not allow myself to fall in love with words. I fall in love with the performances and images. The script is nothing more than a means of communicating with my cast, my crew, and with the people who are putting up the dough."

The most recent instance of James Cameron writing a screenplay that he was not to direct was *Strange Days*, the noisy Twentieth Century Fox film that was ultimately directed by Cameron's third wife, Kathryn Bigelow. *Strange Days* is about the last night of the twentieth century. Lenny Nero (Ralph Fiennes) is an ex-cop who peddles data discs that contain real emotions and memories of others that can be experienced by people who play them on an apparatus they strap onto their heads.

Lenny was a lousy cop and is an even more pathetic criminal (most of these discs contain illegal activity that provides the user with a vicarious thrill), but there are things that he simply will not do. He generally refuses to deal in discs that feature "snuff" or portray murder and rape, but he finds himself in heaps of trouble both with the police and with the underworld when he comes into possession of a disc that shows police beating and killing a black rap star. Lenny becomes a moving target for the police, who do not want the public to see what is on the disc, and the gangsters, who don't want the disc traced back to them.

Cameron thought up and started working on this idea in 1985, a full ten years before it got to the screen, and seven years before the Rodney King videotape and the Los Angeles riots of 1992 that his story so eerily predicts.

Cameron's intention in *Strange Days* was to write a moody thriller that takes place on New Year's Eve, 1999. He was fascinated with the dramatic and thematic potential of the end of the millennium. He wanted the impending doomsday to serve as a backdrop for the redemption of one individual. The movie was conceived as pure *film noir* — even the name of the lead character, Nero, is Italian for black.

Cameron's outline for *Strange Days* took up five handwritten pages. Between the outline and the screenplay completed in 1994, very little of the storyline changed. Sometime in 1992 Cameron pitched the idea to director Kathryn Bigelow. He was beginning to worry that the end of the millennium was drawing too close for the film to be considered science fiction. Although he had intended to direct the movie himself, his commitments to *True Lies* and other projects precluded this. He was willing to let the cherished screenplay go only to a director whom he completely trusted. He had worked with Bigelow when he served as executive producer and writer (uncredited) on her *Point Break* (1991), a strangely misguided movie about some surfers who rob banks to finance their carefree lifestyle.

Cameron had first met Kathryn Bigelow in 1989 when he visited the set of her film *Blue Steel* (1990) to speak to the star of the film, Jamie Lee Curtis, about playing the female lead in *True Lies*. Bigelow is an exciting filmmaker. Her movies are visually rich and gloriously stylish. She started her artistic career as a painter, then switched to moviemaking after studying film at Columbia University. Her first film, a 1950s biker-style movie starring Willem Dafoe called *Loveless* (1983), shows Bigelow to be a director to be reckoned with. She followed up with a terrific vampire movie, *Near Dark* (1987), and then with *Blue Steel*, a dark movie about a rookie policewoman (Curtis) having to deal with the sexism of her male colleagues, and with a maniacal stalker who has picked her as the target for his dangerously delusional affections. Bigelow's talents earned her a career retrospective at the Museum of Modern Art in 1990. She became James Cameron's third wife right after completing *Blue Steel* in 1989.

When asked about the level of violence that is common in her films, a level that is usually associated with male action directors, Bigelow calmly replies that she has never once portrayed violence in any of her movies as anything other than ugly. She persuasively argues that the street torture of truck driver Reginald Denny during the Los Angeles riots was far more brutal than anything she would show in her films.

Bigelow liked Cameron's idea for *Strange Days* and agreed to wait until he had fully fleshed it out in a screenplay. Cameron soon realized that his ambitious outline would require him to write a screenplay that was more character driven and more densely plotted than anything he had ever attempted before. "I wanted Elmore Leonard to come to me like Elvis came to Christian Slater in *True*

Romance and tell me how to do this shit," remembers Cameron. As he struggled, Bigelow's patience started wearing thin. She was turning projects down as she waited for him. His eight years of vague ideas, three months of focused pondering, four weeks of writing, and a few days of intense cramming produced what Cameron describes as a "two-headed calf," something that was neither a screenplay nor a treatment. The intention was to write a 30- or 40-page treatment; what he ended up with was a 131-page hybrid.

At this point Cameron simply ran out of time — the *True Lies* start date was zooming toward him. He hired Jay Cocks to write the shooting screenplay for *Strange Days* for him. Cocks, a former *Time* magazine movie critic, is a favorite collaborator of Martin Scorsese, having written *The Last Temptation of Christ* and *The Age of Innocence* with the famed director. The results are intriguing and hyperkinetic, but in the end unsatisfying. Ralph Fiennes (*The English Patient*), who stars as Lenny Nero, is a brilliant actor but seems uncomfortable in the middle of this big American action movie. With its noisy street violence, rampant corruption, and profound pessimism, *Strange Days* paints a bleak picture of urban life at the dawn of the twenty-first century.

James Cameron has been criticized for his alleged weakness as a screenwriter time and time again. Nevertheless, when you read a James Cameron screenplay through, you are immediately struck by the density of the descriptions.

His scenes are described in great detail, his characters are well thought out, and the dialogue suits the characters' personalities. His latest screenplay, *Titanic*, is no exception; in fact, it may be the finest writing he has ever done. The story is moving and the characters are compelling. For someone who despises writing with as much vitriol as James Cameron, he certainly has a talent for it. Perhaps the problem is that Cameron has two sides to his creative imagination. When he writes he pours everything he has into the screenplay, but when he gets on the set the hugeness of the undertaking assumes priority over the nuances of the story.

Five

MAKING *THE* TERMINATOR

"There's no fate but what we make for ourselves."

"SARAH CONNOR" IN *THE TERMINATOR*

Los Angeles, 1984. A garbage collector is working the night shift. A weird electrical disturbance shuts his vehicle down completely. A ball of crackling electricity appears and gives birth to a hulking, naked, human-looking being, which strolls toward some loitering punks and demands their clothes. When the punks (one played by Bill Paxton in his first movie appearance) laughingly rebuke him, the Terminator, played by Arnold Schwarzenegger, dispatches

them. One unfortunate creep has a fist literally shoved
through his chest. Needless to say, the Terminator walks
away fully dressed.

Cut to a debris-strewn alleyway, where a second ball of
static electricity leaves another naked, groaning figure in
its wake. He is Reese (Michael Biehn). The police come
upon Reese, and he flees. The foot chase through the back
alleys of L.A. is shot with such style that we are sucked
right into the screen. Reese manages to evade the police
and heads to a telephone booth where he urgently looks
up the name Sarah Connor. It is now the next day and we
are watching a plain-looking young woman, Sarah Connor
(Linda Hamilton), ride her motorscooter to her job as a
waitress at a small fast-food restaurant. At the same time
the Terminator is visiting a local gunshop, where he arms
himself with a frightening arsenal of automatic weapons.
He then heads to a telephone booth, where he tears out the
page of the directory containing the "Connor, Sarah" listing.
He goes to visit the first Sarah Connor on the list, who is
not the waitress, and kills her with stone-faced indifference.

Reese takes refuge in a car and falls asleep. Through
his dreams we are given a glimpse of the world he came
from, a place of apocalyptic desolation where a ragtag army
of men battle huge laser-spouting machines. He awakens
with a start as we cut to two detectives scanning the reports
of a bizarre coincidence. Two women named Sarah Connor
have been brutally murdered within hours of each other.

Our Sarah Connor is at home getting ready for a date. When her date stands her up she decides to go out anyway because her roommate has invited her boyfriend over for the evening. Unbeknownst to Sarah, the police are desperately trying to reach her because she is the next Sarah Connor in the phone book. She is in a bar when she sees a newscast describing the Sarah Connor murders. Alarmed, and suddenly feeling that she is being followed, she heads out onto the street. She ducks into the nearest door, a nightclub called Tech Noir, where she calls the police.

The Terminator goes to Sarah's house and kills the roommate and her boyfriend, believing the young woman to be Sarah. Before he leaves, the Terminator hears a frantic Sarah leaving a message on the answering machine. She says that she is at Tech Noir and needs help.

Sarah manages to reach the two detectives investigating the case and they tell her to stay put. But the Terminator gets there ahead of them. So does Reese. The Terminator finds Sarah in the crowd and aims his laser-sighted automatic pistol at her. Before he can fire, Reese blasts him repeatedly with a shotgun he took from a police car. Reese then grabs Sarah, saying, "Come with me if you want to live!"

The seemingly indestructible Terminator gives chase, but the pair elude him in a car that Reese has stolen. Reese explains that he is here to protect Sarah because she has been targeted for termination. He explains that they are being pursued by a Terminator, a cybernetic organism unleashed from the future. Sarah asks, "Why me?" and Reese tells her that after the nuclear war that will occur in a few decades, a war started by the supercomputers, there was one man who taught the remaining people to rise up and fight against the machines. His name is John Connor, and he is Sarah's unborn son.

The Terminator finds them and another vicious car chase and gunfight ensue, with the result that Sarah and Reese are taken into police custody. Sarah tells a police psychologist everything that Reese has told her. Reese in turn is questioned by the police psychiatrist. He answers all the questions, without suspecting that they think he is crazy. The Terminator has only one purpose, he explains: finding Sarah Connor.

Meanwhile, in a downtown flophouse, the Terminator, who has been injured during the previous gunfight and chase, does some gruesomely graphic autosurgery to repair his damaged components. He then arms himself to the teeth and heads to the police station to fulfill the prophecy outlined by Reese. It is at the police station that the robotic Arnold Schwarzenegger utters the famous phrase "I'll be back," just before he slaughters almost everybody in the place in a sequence of stark and brutal violence. Reese and Sarah manage to escape, and they take refuge under a bridge, where Sarah tends to his wounded arm. Reese tells her more about her unborn son and the dark fate that awaits humanity in the not-too-distant future. The next morning they head deeper into the countryside and, they hope, farther away from the Terminator. They check into a motel and prepare for their next move.

Reese and Sarah share some tender moments together, and make love in a scene that is remarkably poignant, given the overall nature of the movie. Their conjunction sets up the interesting premise that Reese is the father of the future resistance leader John Connor — who had to send him back in time to ensure that he will actually exist.

Just as we are lulled into a mellow postcoital mood, the Terminator arrives on a Harley and all hell breaks loose. Another high-intensity car/motorcycle chase tears across the screen. Reese is shot before the pickup truck that he and Sarah are driving flips and rolls over. The Terminator's motorcycle is hit by a huge gasoline-loaded tanker truck. The indestructible Terminator climbs to his feet and violently commandeers the truck with the intention of running down the fleeing, injured couple. Reese and Sarah separate to confuse the Terminator. Reese lodges a homemade pipe bomb in the rear of the transport, causing it to explode in an enormous fireball that rains fire down from the sky for as far as we can see. The Terminator is trapped inside.

Sarah and Reese reunite and collapse in relief amid a sea of flames. In the background we see the shining metal endoskeleton of the Terminator rising up from the wreckage of the truck. The endoskeleton continues the pursuit into a nearby factory. Reese is able to plant his one remaining pipe bomb in the endoskeleton, blowing it to pieces. When the air has cleared, Sarah is horrified to discover that Reese was killed in the blast.

Just when you think the horror has finally come to an end, Cameron terrorizes his audience even further by having the top half of the Terminator endoskeleton crawl toward Sarah across the floor of the factory. Sarah appears to be cornered by the advancing nightmare, until she realizes that she has lured the Terminator onto a heavy metal press, which she activates, crushing whatever "life" remains in the robot. The movie ends with the pregnant Sarah heading off to the rugged wilds of Mexico. She stops to get gas and remarks to a boy there that she is in a hurry because "there is a storm coming."

All in all, *The Terminator* represents a huge leap forward for director James Cameron. It can be likened to the leap that Quentin Tarantino made from *Reservoir Dogs* to *Pulp Fiction* or that Scottish director Danny Boyle made from *Shallow Grave* to *Trainspotting*, except that Cameron's directorial debut wasn't remarkable in the least. He proved with *The Terminator* that he could write and direct a decent action movie with solid confidence.

The genesis of *The Terminator* lay in the fever-induced images that Cameron experienced when he was in Rome during the post-production of *Piranha 2*. He later sketched the images that were burned into his consciousness during the dream, something he often does. "The sketch was of a half Terminator, which actually looks pretty much like the finished one. He is crawling after a girl who is injured and cannot get up and run. The Terminator is pulling himself along using a kitchen knife, dragging a broken arm. It was really a horrific image."

This dream inspired Cameron to sit down and outline a screenplay about a robot hitman from the future. When he finally got back to Los Angeles and *Piranha 2: The Spawning* was completed, he was ready to move on to his next project. When he pitched the robot hitman story to his agent, he met an unenthusiastic response. "His response was 'Bad idea, bad idea, don't waste your time, work on something else.' What I did was fire him and start writing."

As he wrote out idea after idea he found himself throwing aspects of his own life into the mix. He gave his female lead the same job that his first wife, Sarah, had had, a waitress. His wife had worked at Bob's Big Boy. In *The Terminator* Sarah Connor works at Bob's Big Buns. He even cast a yappy little dog in the movie that was just like the one he had when he was sharing a tiny house with his first wife. Cameron's marriage was now all but over; he had become firmly possessed by his work as a moviemaker. Success — his version of success — was all that he had his eye on.

By 1983 Cameron was living in a small one-bedroom apartment in Tarzana, California, and he was writing with a partner of sorts, Gale Anne Hurd. Cameron had worked with Hurd briefly at New World, and she was now striking out to produce movies on her own through her company, Pacific Western Productions. She was taken by Cameron's enthusiasm and drive and by his ability to generate exciting ideas. Their script was a solid 130 pages rich with strange characters mixed with everyday people and replete with striking images. Once the screenplay was done Cameron sold it to Hurd for the princely sum of one dollar, which allowed her to take it to the studios and set it up for Cameron to direct, as was stipulated in their partnership agreement. *The Terminator* was shopped around to every movie studio in town and was turned down just as quickly by every one of them. Then it landed on the desk of upstart British producer John Daly at Hemdale Pictures.

The son of a Cockney dockworker, Daly dropped out of school at fifteen and spent some time in the merchant marine before returning to London, where he became an insurance salesman. One day he had a chance encounter with actor David Hemmings and the two struck up a friendship. This friendship led to a partnership in a talent agency they called Hemdale. Before long they were successfully involved in music, TV, and movie representation. In 1971 Daly bought out Hemmings's share and moved Hemdale to Hollywood.

His involvement in *The Terminator* would catapult Daly into the big time. He would later share in an Oscar win in 1986 for producing *Platoon* with Oliver Stone and then helped arrange the financing for Bernardo Bertolucci's wonderful *Last Emperor*. When Daly read *The Terminator* screenplay he was intrigued and wanted to meet James Cameron to discuss it further. Cameron knew he had to make this pitch unique and memorable, so he enlisted the help of his pal Lance Henriksen, whom he entertained thoughts of casting as the Terminator. Henriksen has a clear memory of this near-legendary pitch meeting. "There is a great story behind that. I went into Hemdale, and Jim had planned it so I would get there about half an hour ahead of him. I went in decked out like the Terminator. I put gold foil from the Vantage cigarette package in my teeth and waxed my hair back. Jim had put fake cuts on my head. I wore a ripped-up punk rock T shirt, a leather jacket, and boots up to my knees. It was really an exciting look. I was a scary person to be in a room with. I kicked the door open when I got there and the poor secretary just about swallowed her typewriter. I headed in to see the producer. I sat in the room with him and I wouldn't talk to him. I just kept looking at him. After a few minutes of that he was ready to jump out the window."

Cameron brought up the rear with an enthusiastic pitch that included detailed sketches of various sequences in the screenplay. Daly was dazzled by the fledgling director's passion and impressed by the sketches, which inspired confidence in Cameron's ability to actually put his idea on the screen. Cameron had already shot this movie in his head and it showed. Daly decided to back the movie with the resources of his Hemdale Films. He would later make a distribution deal with Orion Pictures to limit his own financial exposure.

Cameron's first preoccupation was the casting of Reese, the heroic warrior from the future who comes back to give his life to ensure the survival of humanity. The role of the Terminator was considered secondary: he was just a robot, after all.

One night at one of an endless number of Hollywood parties, Orion Pictures co-founder Mike Medavoy ran into an up-and-coming bodybuilder-cum-actor by the name of Arnold Schwarzenegger. Medavoy told Schwarzenegger about *The Terminator*, mentioning that the lead had not been cast yet. He arranged for Schwarzenegger to read the screenplay. The actor reacted to the screenplay with a degree of confusion. "Mike told me about *The Terminator*," Schwarzenegger recalls. "He said that the movie didn't have a leading man, so when I read the script it was with that in mind. I read the script thinking that I might like to play Reese."

Arnold Schwarzenegger was born in Graz, Austria, the son of the local police chief. He went against his father's wishes when at age fifteen he decided that he wanted a career as a bodybuilder rather than as a professional soccer player. Before long he was crowned Junior Mr. Europe.

He would go on to win the Mr. World title, the Mr. Olympia title seven times, and the Mr. Universe title five times. Schwarzenegger started a mail order business dealing in health products and invested his profits wisely, becoming a millionaire while he was still in his twenties. He then decided that he wanted to try his hand at acting.

Inspired by Steve Reeves and his Hercules films, the young Austrian took the stage name of Arnold Strong and appeared in the cheesy action movie *Hercules in New York* in 1970, for which his lines were dubbed. But it wasn't until 1976 that people would start taking notice of Schwarzenegger, after he appeared in George Butler's fascinating documentary on the bodybuilding subculture called *Pumping Iron*. He attracted the attention of director Bob Rafelson, who was then casting his eccentric character study *Stay Hungry* with Jeff Bridges and Sally Field. In his first speaking role, Schwarzenegger played a reigning Mr. Austria in America desperately trying to raise money to pay off a debt to a gym owner. *Stay Hungry* would actually win Arnold an acting award: he won the Golden Globe for Most Promising Newcomer. Schwarzenegger was then cast in the comedy western *The Villain* (1979) opposite Kirk Douglas and Ann-Margret, where he was essentially the joke of the project. His real break would come in his next movie, when director John Milius cast him in his version of Robert E. Howard's fantasy novel series, *Conan the Barbarian*, in 1981. The dark and violent *Terminator* was a different animal from any of Schwarzenegger's previous films.

James Cameron was skeptical. The studio was suggesting that Arnold Schwarzenegger be cast in the role of Reese and a former football hero turned actor named O.J. Simpson be cast as the Terminator — an uncomfortable irony, given Simpson's future notoriety as the prime suspect in the double murder of his wife, Nicole, and waiter Ron Goldman. Cameron was concerned about the imposing nature of Schwarzenegger's physique. If Schwarzenegger were to play a good guy, then someone of truly gargantuan proportions would have to be cast as the villain to be even semi-believable. Upon meeting, however, Schwarzenegger and Cameron hit it off. As they discussed the project, Schwarzenegger kept harking back to the robotic Terminator and what an interesting idea it was. "I kept saying that he had to be able to change weapons blindfolded and shoot guns without blinking his eyes, and how he should walk with his head tilted forward," Schwarzenegger remembers. "Jim finally just said, 'You should play the Terminator.' I was a bit surprised. I told him, 'I came in here for the other part.'"

Cameron whipped out a pad and pencil and started sketching furiously. Looking back, he says, "My initial intent was to make a film like *Alien*, which, even though it was a science fiction film, was still done with a sense of the immediate, an almost documentary realism. The Terminator was going to be a guy with a scary face but not physically imposing. I intended him to be a sort of lurking figure in the crowd, with the collar of his trenchcoat turned up like a guy in a *film noir*. But once Arnold was cast, the complexion of the film changed completely. Gritty realism would never have worked with Arnold in the role."

Cameron retooled his notions of what the Terminator was to look like. Not Lance Henriksen, not German actor Jürgen Prochnow, whom he considered briefly. Cameron is a huge fan of the German film *Das Boot*, in which Prochnow played the captain of a Nazi U-boat. He loves the way director Wolfgang Petersen made each scene in the film purposeful and well thought out. He thought the casting of Prochnow would have made *The Terminator* more intense and introspective, not qualities that anyone would attribute to O.J. Simpson. However, when all was said and done, Arnold Schwarzenegger *was* the Terminator.

Today Schwarzenegger is full of support for the film that made him a star, but he was considerably less enthusiastic when he signed for the movie. Journalist Rick Wayne interviewed him while he was making *Conan the Destroyer*. When asked about an unusual pair of boots sitting near them, Schwarzenegger commented, "Oh, those are from some shit movie I'm doing for a couple of weeks." On another occasion he was quoted as saying, "I don't know what kind of crazy movie this is, they're from outer space and they are shooting each other, they shoot each other every minute, it's crazy."

The actor left out of the mix was Cameron's friend Lance Henriksen, who had played a role in helping get the project up and running. To his credit, Henriksen took this exclusion with great class and professionalism. Cameron felt both grateful and indebted to Henriksen for all he had done, and he made sure that he was given a role in the movie, albeit a considerably smaller one.

Lance Henriksen responds evenly when asked about being passed over for the role. "I never for one second felt that Jim Cameron shortchanged me. I've learned enough about this business over the years to realize that this is just the way it goes sometimes. I wanted Jim to get the movie made just as much as I wanted to be in it. So it really didn't hurt at all. Then another role in the movie came up, one of the cops, and Jim asked me if I wanted it. I jumped at the chance to be in his movie in any role that he offered me." But as Henriksen continues to describe his feelings on *The Terminator* it is evident that he did, at one time, think about being the Terminator. "If I had played the Terminator it would have been a much different movie. It wouldn't have been such a physical character, it would have been much more of a mental character."

A lot of second-guessing was swirling around the casting of Schwarzenegger in the role and around the movie itself. James Cameron, on the other hand, never doubted the potential of what he was doing, and had great faith in the character's box-office appeal. "Strangely, I think people root for the Terminator because deep down inside all of us there lurks a person who would love to be like him, even if just for two minutes. Everyone would like to walk into the boss's office without using the doorknob."

To prepare for the role of the Terminator, Schwarzenegger went to shooting ranges for three months and trained with every form of firearm available. He went not only to learn how to shoot the weapons but also to become comfortable around the sounds of gunfire.

By the time the film went into production everyone knew that casting Arnold Schwarzenegger had been the perfect thing to do. One of the strongly supportive voices came from cinematographer Adam Greenberg. "Right from the start I knew we had something in Arnold Schwarzenegger. He's got great cheekbones, very strong and powerful. I used harsh top lighting to pick up the high-lights and spread the shadows evenly beneath. I also wanted to make him look larger than life, more powerful, so I would shoot him from below using wide-angle lenses to distort him."

Although Schwarzenegger's looks were key to the movie, his acting ability was never overestimated. Cameron knew just what he was getting but he was confident that the odd angularity of Schwarzenegger's face, combined with his powerful physique, would create an image that people would remember. Cameron was excited by Schwarzenegger's potential in the role, but soon discovered he would have to put his eagerness to get started on hold. Schwarzenegger was contractually obligated to star in the sequel to *Conan the Barbarian*, called *Conan the Destroyer*, before he would be free to make *The Terminator*. He would not be available for at least four months if all went according to schedule. Cameron went back to his sketch pad and accepted the writing assignments for *Rambo: First Blood Part II* and *Aliens*.

As the proposed start date for *The Terminator* drew nearer and nearer, Cameron was overwhelmed by a child-like enthusiasm for every aspect of the project. He proudly showed off the sketches he had been doing to anyone he was trying to enlist as cast or crew.

The start date arrived on February 8, 1984. Cameron arrived on the set like a seasoned professional and quickly established himself as an encyclopedia of cinematic technology and a demanding perfectionist. Arnold Schwarzenegger was dazzled by Cameron when work began. "You should have seen him. He would line up his shots so precisely in advance that if it ended up being a half inch off the way he planned it he would go completely berserk," the star recalls.

Cameron tried to impress upon his cast and crew that he was not a foot-stomping megalomaniac or a mega-phone-wielding Hollywood prima donna. He was willing to explain every decision he made and he won everyone over with his approachability and willingness to put him-self on the line. Schwarzenegger was impressed by

Cameron's ability to take risks and give himself over to the job at hand. He says, "I remember Jim coming onto the set to shoot some stunts — they were physical stunts. Jim demonstrated them himself. He did the stunts without padding and without seemingly giving it another thought. There were times during that shoot that I really thought to myself that he was completely fucking crazy."

As shooting progressed some of the cast and crew members wondered whether Cameron was a trifle too obsessed with his project. The seeds of his reputation for being excessively demanding were sown on this film. Schwarzenegger was often witness to his strange behavior. "He was so blunt at times. I would do a scene and would ask him how it was. He'd say something like, 'It was disastrous, but probably a human being could do no worse.' He was talking to me like I *was* the Terminator. It got pretty freaky at times."

With his surefooted direction of *The Terminator*, Cameron asserted himself as a filmmaker who was not afraid of huge set pieces, complex stunts, and visual excitement. For the explosion of the tanker truck, it took a full three months to set up the street with models and a miniature truck. The shot was covered by three cameras. The first attempt at the explosion failed miserably. The crew, including pyrotechnic expert Joe Viskocil, had to redo the scene and they didn't have long to do it. Three months to set up the first take was reduced to one week to set up the second and necessarily last take. Miraculously, it all came together while the entire cast and crew held their collective breath.

The groundbreaking effects in *The Terminator* came from James Cameron's imagination and from the talents of effects designer Stan Winston. Winston came to Hollywood from his native West Virginia with the intention of becoming an actor, but after working as an apprentice at Walt Disney studios in 1969 he realized that he could create more interesting characters using makeup effects. He won an Emmy award with his partner Rick Baker for the astounding age makeup applied to Cicely Tyson for her lead role in *The Autobiography of Miss Jane Pittman* in 1974. When Cameron approached him about creating the effects for *The Terminator*, he had just completed work on a low-budget horror movie called *Parasite*.

Because of the nature of some of the effects shots in *The Terminator* Winston was somewhat boggled. He was told he had a limited budget but that he would be required to create convincing, full-sized robotic endoskeletons and human prosthetic devices. A lot of Cameron's shots were designed to be long and lingering, so the pressure was on Winston to create a lifelike representation of Arnold Schwarzenegger. Winston's talents were especially challenged in the memorable sequence where the injured Terminator performs surgery on himself in front of a mirror.

Realizing this shot was long and extremely complex. Stan Winston explained how they did it. "We usually make a life cast of the actor, then make several latex pieces from that casting when they are needed. But a life cast is only an impression, not an exact likeness. When you are taking an impression a certain amount of distortion inevitably takes place. The weight of the impression material pulls the face down, flattening out the expressions and really removing the facial detail of the actor. For this movie I had to use the impression as a starting point. I then took a series of photographs of Arnold making a variety of different facial expressions. I used the photos to resculpt the entire face in clay and I made silicone molds of the sculptures. I then laid in a layer of ultracal, a very hard, quick-drying plaster. Next, we removed the ultracal core and the clay. The ultracal core then fit back inside the silicone mold, leaving a void that is the exact thickness of skin. I then injected foam into that void to produce a very lifelike facial reproduction."

Cameron worked closely with Winston. "Stan Winston wanted, as I did, to make the definitive movie robot," says Cameron. "We both knew from the start that it would end up being an incredibly detailed and complex puppet. There was no way we could do the robot as a man in a suit. It was supposed to be a skeleton, so you have to be able to see through it in places. We had to see more of it than, say, the alien in *Alien*. We couldn't leave it in the shadows and cover it with quick cuts. There had to be enough of it on screen to sustain the massive image that the Terminator had been throughout the entire movie."

Although it was Cameron's intent to give Winston full creative license in creating the robots, he did submit several of his own sketches as points of departure. Winston was immediately taken by the brilliance of the sketches and decided not to alter them in the least. Winston explains, "Jim happens to be an incredible artist, which is great for me because most of the time my biggest problem is working with directors who have no artistic concept whatsoever. Usually I do my own design work, but in this case there was already a concept that was really quite brilliant and I didn't want to change it. Jim's idea was for the robot to appear as organic as possible."

The robot took six months to build with seven people working constantly on it (Michael Mills, Shane Mahan, Tom Woodruff, John Rosengrant, Richard Landon, Brian Wade, and David Miller). Winston explains the rather complex process. "Each of the robot parts was originally sculpted of Roma clay, then molded in gray tuffy, which is a polysulfide flexible rubber compound. Plaster copies were then brought out of these molds. The finished work was done on those plaster castings, which were finely sanded to give them a machined look. Then the plaster castings were molded in BJB 430 urethane, with the final epoxy castings being brought out of those urethane molds. The epoxy castings were composed of an initial coat of epoxy, then a fiberglass cloth coat, then another layer of epoxy. To give the castings strength, we embedded custom-fit steel ribbing into them, and filled them with solid epoxy. The final pieces were then finely sanded, vacuumed, metalized, and painted down to give them a distressed look. One of the reasons that the robot looked so real and seemed so massive and heavy in his movements is because he was that heavy." Because of the steel ribbing that was added to each of the robot's pieces, the Terminator puppet ended up weighing in excess of one hundred pounds. This initially created a problem for the puppeteer who had to manipulate the robot, but the on-screen results are terrifyingly realistic.

Any of the scenes that showed the full robot walking required the use of stop-motion photography. To lessen the potential gaps in continuity that using a full-sized robot and a miniature stop-motion puppet in the same scene might cause, model maker Doug Beswick constructed a two-foot-tall Terminator robot to look as identical to its full-sized cousin as he could make it. "Because of scheduling we built our two-foot version as the full-sized robot was being constructed. I worked very closely with Stan Winston. As soon as he finished a piece we copied it exactly, only on a scale one-third the size," says Beswick.

Once the robots were completed they were chrome-plated for added authenticity. A radio-control mechanism was installed in the head of the large robot to govern its movements.

For the final shot of the Terminator being crushed Winston needed to find a material that would collapse rather than shatter. He ended up using a polyurethane compound that looks exactly like metal when it is being crushed but is only half the weight and cost of metal.

Cameron was delighted with his finished movie. There had been very little compromise and an enormous amount of hellishly hard work, but Cameron believed that he had finally made a film that showcased his talents. It came as a shock to him when Orion Pictures executives, who Cameron thought would flip for his movie, seemed completely indifferent to it. Cameron wearily recalls, "This guy from Orion was downright dismissive of the movie. He told me that a down-and-dirty little action thriller like this usually lasts about three weeks. Box office drops by 50 percent by the second week and then it completely vanishes by the third."

When *The Terminator* opened, it took the number-one spot for the weekend box-office returns and it received some extraordinarily strong reviews from the major critics. *Variety* described the movie as "slick rather nasty but undeniably compelling comic book adventure." One of Canada's foremost critics, the late Jay Scott, wrote in the *Globe and Mail*, "The casting of bodybuilder Arnold Schwarzenegger as a cyborg terminator — a computer gunslinger encased in an envelope of 'living human tissue' — who pops into 1984 from 2029 to kill the mother of a hero of the future so the hero can never be born, is brilliant. In *The Terminator*, a lot of the action takes place in a dance bar, Tech Noir. That describes the bar, the action, and the movie."

Cameron felt somewhat vindicated by audiences' and critics' reactions, but Orion Pictures didn't change their stance. "I really was astounded by their reaction. Even after the initial success, which was even more than I expected, they still had no interest in beefing up the ad campaign or giving it any added support at all. They treated me like dogshit."

The wave of success and vindication that Cameron was feeling would be shortlived. *The Terminator* was doing spectacularly well at the box office, and James Cameron was the talk of the town. Then he and Orion Pictures were blindsided by a lawsuit that came about when the outspoken and prolific science fiction writer Harlan Ellison decided to take in a movie one sunny afternoon. The movie he chose was *The Terminator*. "I loved the movie, was just blown away by it," recalls Ellison. "I walked out of the theater, went home, and called my lawyer."

Ellison claimed that Cameron had based his screenplay on two episodes of the old *Outer Limits* TV series that Ellison had written, "Soldier" and "Demon with the Glass Hand," as well as on a piece of short fiction entitled "I Have No Mouth and I Must Scream." All three concerned time travel and the altering of the past to save humanity from global nuclear catastrophe. They also featured a future inhabited by killer robots.

Harlan Ellison was combative on the issue but he was not angry or vindictive. "He got all my best stuff, but the wonderful thing, he combined it in a new, fresh, interesting way. I would have been flattered. All he had to do was pick up the phone."

James Cameron objected strenuously to Ellison's charges, arguing that time travel and robots are common science fiction themes and numerous other movies, books, TV shows, and comic strips had followed the same thematic lines. Initially Orion and Hemdale gave Cameron the option of fighting the suit, but if Ellison was to win they promised to turn around and sue Cameron. Orion and Hemdale were eager to avoid a public and costly fight. In the end, prints of *The Terminator* were reissued with a credit acknowledging that the works of Harlan Ellison were drawn upon in making the movie. Ellison was also given approximately $400,000 in compensation. Cameron remains bitter about the whole ordeal. "What it came down to was, I could risk getting completely wiped out or I could wave it off and let this guy get his fucking credit."

When all is said and done, it remains a fact that Cameron made a classic movie when he made *The Terminator.* It is a gory, violent action movie with a touching love story at the core. The relationship between Reese and Sarah made the film popular with female audiences, something virtually unheard of in this genre. "The Terminator" along with several lines of dialogue in the movie instantly became part of the popular lexicon. The film catapulted the career of Arnold Schwarzenegger into mega-stardom and he knows it. "No matter what I did after that," says Hollywood's highest-paid star, "people always come up to me and ask me, when are you going to do another Terminator?"

By 1984 Cameron had been working with Gale Anne Hurd for four years. During the development of *The Terminator* a more personal relationship began to develop. One night during this time Cameron took Hurd to a restaurant in Malibu, where the long working relationship turned into a romance. Gale Anne Hurd describes her first "date" with James Cameron as memorable: "We went off-road in a four-wheel-drive vehicle, we went up in a hot air balloon and a huge wind came up causing us to crash land. We went horseback riding, ice skating. We shot AK-47s out in the desert. And that was just in one weekend."

As the romance grew the game playing between the two intensified. When they were scheduled to go to a meeting together they traveled separately, Hurd in her Porsche and Cameron in his new Corvette (bought with his *Terminator* fee), and raced along to the meeting talking to one another on their cellular phones the whole time. For Cameron it was just another thrill to liven up a ride to work. "We'd be smoking down the highway at about 120 miles per hour talking on the phone like nothing out of the ordinary was happening," Cameron remembers with a laugh.

Gale Anne Hurd would soon become the second Mrs. James Cameron.

After completing *The Terminator* but before the movie was released in theaters, Cameron began to express impatience with his growing reputation as a genre filmmaker. "I think it is important to avoid being regarded as the Stephen King of the film world and have everyone know exactly what to expect from you next. I'd like to be in a position where I could do a film like *Terms of Endearment* or *Flashdance* — a more thoughtful version of it, perhaps, but with the same sort of visual dynamic. At the same time I would still like to do the ultimate science fiction film — if such a thing exists."

Cameron would have to wait a full ten years before the opportunity would present itself to direct a mainstream picture like *True Lies*. He made a serious attempt at a movie called *The Crowded Room*, based on the Billy Milligan case concerning a rapist on trial using the multiple-personality defense, but it never came to fruition. It would not be until 1996 and *Titanic* that James Cameron would make a historical romance.

Many times, especially in the modern era, a movie comes out at precisely the right time to tap into the *zeitgeist* and become an enormous hit. It can be a small film, like *Flashdance*, or a blockbuster like *Independence Day*. When audiences look at the same movie a few years later they often wonder just what all the fuss was about. *The*

Terminator fits into the opposite category. More than a decade after its release, *The Terminator* still holds up solidly. Everything from Brad Fiedel's eerie electronic score to the stylishness with which Cameron made the movie are still fresh. Cameron looks back on the film this way: "In some ways *The Terminator* was the ultimate experience for me. I got to conceive the idea, write the screenplay, have a deal made, storyboard the major scenes, go about creating those images in casting and sets and location, then I filmed it. To compare the finished product to the storyboard and seeing a satisfyingly similar image is for me a clean sweep. I got to do everything I wanted to do."

Cameron tried to construct a movie that would succeed on several levels. He wanted equally to impress twelve-year-old boys with nonstop action and high-impact special effects and to inspire fifty-year-old film professors to read all kinds of sociopolitical significance into the movie.

That the movie succeeded to the extent that it did even without the support of the home studio, Orion Pictures, makes its outcome even more remarkable. Orion compressed all the ad money into the final week before the release. They held only one preview showing and promoted the film as if it were a *Dirty Harry* knock-off with a science fiction twist. When they wanted the poster to depict a bare-chested Arnold Schwarzenegger to draw in a female audience, Cameron argued that the Terminator was intended to be completely asexual and that women would be attracted to the film by the poignant romance of the two central human characters.

Many viewers and critics have cited *The Terminator*'s surprising humor. The screenplay contains many funny lines that are delivered in a droll, deadpan manner by Schwarzenegger. But humor and cheekiness were also the tools many reviewers chose to tackle discussions of the film. Suspense novelist and Baltimore *Sun* film reviewer Stephen Hunter wrote, "This high-tech, gun-crazy nightmare is calculated to drive pointy heads, secular humanists, wimp liberals, and other quiche-eaters apoplectic with rage, while yanking in millions at the box office ... and it features the best action sequences to come down the pike since *The Road Warrior*." Later in his piece he praises Cameron's work while deriding the film itself. "Give it to James Cameron, who directed and co-wrote: He'll never win either the Nobel Prize for Literature or Peace, but he knows how to turn an audience on. A superb action mechanic, Cameron delivers a sense of rocketing pace and terrifying plausibility that keeps the film flying along even when its plot permutations are absurd or predictable. *The Terminator* is as violent as a cockfight, but of its sleazy kind, it's terrific, a new trashclassic."

The Terminator is one of those movies that people love to hate and hate to love. It offends with its violence and nihilism but at the same time it succeeds on all levels as a piece of action filmmaking. *The Terminator* got people talking in Hollywood. They wondered about James Cameron. Could he deliver consistently on the promise that he had demonstrated with his first major film? He was about to answer them.

Six

ALIENS: THIS TIME IT'S WAR

"I think it is probably safe to say that if I had been offered Aliens *before* The Terminator *came out, I probably would have shied away from it."*

JAMES CAMERON

James Cameron had been working hard on the screenplay for a sequel to the 1979 Twentieth Century Fox hit *Alien* before he started work on *The Terminator*. Word of Cameron's talent started to spread. Stories of the dedication he demonstrated on the making of the B-movie *Piranha 2: The Spawning* started to filter down. He was another Roger Corman alumnus and a writer of proven ability who could connect with the popular sensibilities of a wide audience. Producers Walter Hill and David Giler were so impressed with the work that he was showing them on his *Alien 2* screenplay that they suggested he might direct it himself. Cameron thought hard about making this sequel as his next film, then agreed, with the stipulation that his soon-to-be wife and producing partner, Gale Anne Hurd, be brought on board as producer. Twentieth Century Fox and Brandywine Productions (owners of the sequel rights to *Alien*) agreed. The budget was set at a then whopping $18 million.

When James Cameron had first been contacted about what was then called *Alien 2* he went into a meeting with producers Hill and Giler with an open mind. All they told him was, "Ripley and soldiers"; they gave him nothing specific whatsoever to work with. Cameron was receptive to this slim concept because at the time he was also in the early stages of researching and writing *Rambo*, and military ideas and themes were much on his mind. He explains, "I thought the concept of grunts in space was wonderful. There is a whole list of science fiction books dating back to the twenties that involve this, but it really hadn't been tried on film. So I took that idea and all the elements of the first film that I liked and thought would be worth retaining, and from there the story crystallized very quickly. In about two days, as a matter of fact. I just sat down, drank a lot of coffee, and wrote out a treatment." It was while

Cameron was writing *Alien 2* that he got the official green light to make *The Terminator*.

As *The Terminator*'s success started washing over Cameron in early fall of 1984, he tried to do whatever he could to avoid becoming just another flavor of the month. "I think it is probably safe to say that if I had been offered *Aliens* before *The Terminator* came out then I probably would have shied away from it. But it didn't happen that way. I accepted the *Aliens* with the tentative suggestion that I might be allowed to direct the film. When it came time to do *The Terminator*, the *Aliens* screenplay wasn't completely finished yet, but Walter Hill and David Giler decided that since they liked the pages they would wait until after I finished shooting *The Terminator* and let me pick it up there and continue. At that point I didn't really need to do an *Alien* sequel, but I liked what I had created. Once that imagery is in my head I cannot get rid of it any other way but to go out and make the movie. Then I never have to deal with it again."

Alien was released in the summer of 1979 and was critically acclaimed and a moderate hit at the box office. It was an odd science fiction movie about a horrific biomechanical alien life force that is inadvertently brought aboard an outer space mining vessel and the claustrophobic battle the ragtag crew wages with it. It was directed by British filmmaker Ridley Scott. Scott had already made a name for himself in Britain for the technically sophisticated and visually dazzling TV commercials he directed. He turned his attentions to directing for the big screen in 1977 when he made a strange adaptation of the Joseph Conrad short story "The Duellists," about a lifelong rivalry between two soldiers in Napoleon's army, played by Harvey Keitel and Keith Carradine. The movie was stylish and gorgeous to look at even though the script was occasionally confusing. The film went on to win the Cannes Film Festival prize for Best First Film. *Alien* was Scott's second film.

(While Cameron's *Aliens* was in production at Pinewood Studios in England, he ran into Ridley Scott in the hallway. Cameron was taken aback that Scott didn't seem even slightly curious about how work was going on the sequel to the movie that had made his career; instead they talked mainly about the challenges and benefits of filming in England.)

Alien thrilled and chilled audiences all summer long, but it hadn't originally been considered a hot property. It was Twentieth Century Fox president Alan Ladd Jr. who pushed the movie forward. *Alien* went on to take in a healthy but not overly dazzling $60 million.

Cameron found himself facing a tight deadline. On the personal side, he and Gale Anne Hurd had been spending a lot of time together and knew they would be spending even more time together in England during the production of the film. They decided to make it official and get married. This step was also in keeping with a trend in James

Cameron's life, a trend of having his personal life closely linked with his professional life. Since he directed his first film and divorced his first wife, Cameron has been married to a producer, a director, and an actress, all of whom have first been colleagues.

Cameron's *Aliens* screenplay begins fifty-seven years after *Alien* left off. Lieutenant Ripley (Sigourney Weaver) is found drifting in space in a hyper-sleep chamber in the shuttle craft she used to escape the alien. She is taken to the massive Gateway Space Station, where she is restored to good health. She is greeted by a smoothy in a suit and tie named Carter Burke (Paul Reiser), who says he works for "the Company." Ripley is flabbergasted when Burke explains that she has been floating in space for so many years. She is asked to address a court of inquiry as to the true nature of what happened to her mining vessel, the *Nostromo*. Ripley explains the horrors she has been through, starting with the alien life form they picked up on the planet LV426. But the court does not believe her story of an acid-bleeding creature. The leader of the inquiry explains that her story lacks credibility because LV426 has been populated by a colony of terraformers who are transforming the atmosphere into a hospitable environment for human habitation. He adds that sixty or seventy colonist families have been living on the planet for twenty years. Ripley is ordered into psychiatric evaluation.

Something then goes horribly wrong on LV426. Burke

asks Ripley if she will go back to the planet with a group
of Colonial Marines to assist them in a consulting capacity only. At first Ripley flatly refuses, but she is talked into
cooperating.

Aboard the Marine transport vessel Ripley is introduced
to a unit of intergalactic soldiers and a strange character
named Bishop (Lance Henriksen), who describes himself
as an "artificial person" — in other words, an android like
Ash (Ian Holm) who terrorized her aboard the *Nostromo*.
Just before they land, Ripley briefs the Marines on the
nature of the opponent they are about to face. They are
greeted on the surface of the planet with an eerie silence.
All the families seem to have vanished. Ripley comes upon
a laboratory that is filled with her worst nightmare, several
alien creatures floating in glass containers. She also comes
across a little girl named Newt (Carrie Henn), who appears
to be the only surviving colonist. Newt is in the grip of
catatonic terror. As the Marines investigate they find that
the colonists are all in one area, dead, and cocooned to the
walls and ceiling by a kind of resin.

Then the aliens move in. Legions of these biomechanical creatures attack the Marines and a furious firefight
follows. Even though the Marines are well armed and well
trained, they can see that they are up against something
bigger than they are. They regroup and try to figure out
what to do next. Marine leader Hicks (Michael Biehn)
orders the evacuation ship to pick them up and then nuke

the planet. But the evacuation ship crashes before they can be rescued. Left to their own devices, the Marines, Ripley, Newt, and Bishop make their way to a shuttle craft in another part of the compound; they hope to pilot it back to the Marine mothership. But they are again surrounded by aliens. Bishop then reveals that part of the mission was to bring one of the aliens back to Gateway for study by the Company's bio-weapons division.

The aliens attack and the Marines fight valiantly but lose a large number of their team. While Newt is leading Hicks and Ripley through an air duct system to a way out so they can engage the aliens from the rear, she slips and falls between the blades of a fan into a sewer system below. Ripley and Hicks frantically cut through the grating to rescue her, but before they reach her an alien rises up from the water and snatches her away. Hicks and Ripley are confronted by another alien on their way to rescue Newt and Hicks is badly injured in the battle. Ripley forges ahead and discovers that Newt has been partially cocooned in a huge nest of alien eggs. Ruling over the nest is the fourteen-foot-tall alien queen.

Ripley incinerates as many eggs as she can before grabbing Newt and escaping. The alien queen gives chase as they race back to where Bishop is waiting to pick them up in the shuttle vehicle. Just as the alien queen is about to grab them, Ripley and Newt make it aboard and Bishop blasts off. Once Bishop makes it back to the Marine mothership he is torn apart by the alien queen, which had managed to stow away on the spacecraft. Ripley and the alien queen do fierce hand-to-hand battle while Ripley is encased in a power loader, a huge forklift that the user wears like an iron suit. The battle ends with Ripley and the alien queen toppling into an air lock, from whence the alien queen is jettisoned into space once and for all.

Ripley, Newt, what's left of Bishop, and the wounded Hicks seal themselves into their hyper-sleep chambers for the long ride home.

Aliens is a dazzling hold-your-breath rollercoaster ride that grips viewers for two and a half hours. The movie is remarkable for a number of reasons. It is one of those rare sequels that actually equals or betters its original. (*Funny Lady* is a better movie than *Funny Girl, The Godfather Part II* is better than *The Godfather,* and *French Connection II* is better than *The French Connection.*) Sequels tend to be either pale imitations or simple cash grabs. Yet *Aliens* is a big-budget movie with a cast made up of largely unknown actors, with the exception of Sigourney Weaver, whose career was made by playing the same character in *Alien.* Bill Paxton delivers an effective seriocomic performance as a brave Marine who reaches the limit of his valor quickly. Michael Biehn, appearing in his second James Cameron movie in a row, is just the right combination of tough-as-nails Marine and compassionate friend to Ripley. And Paul Reiser is suitably smarmy as a government stooge who cannot tell the truth about anything. (Reiser went on to great success as the co-star and co-creator of the successful TV sitcom *Mad about You.*) Lance Henriksen was also appearing in his second James Cameron movie in a row, as Bishop the android. Cameron asked most of the people with whom he had worked on *The Terminator* to join him again both in front of and behind the camera. This was a trait that he would exhibit throughout his career.

An important element in making *Aliens* was the participation of Sigourney Weaver. After *Alien* put Weaver on the map, she wasted no time in building a solid career for herself. She had appeared in such notable films as *Eyewitness*, *The Year of Living Dangerously*, and *Ghostbusters* before she was approached about *Aliens*. She wasn't predisposed to making *Aliens* just because Ripley was her starmaking role. It had to be good or she wasn't going to sign on.

Sigourney Weaver (born Susan Alexandra Weaver, she borrowed her adopted name from a character in *The Great Gatsby*) grew up in a showbiz family. Her parents are Sylvester "Pat" Weaver, a former president of NBC Television, and Elizabeth Inglis, an actress. Sigourney took up acting at the Yale School of Drama and graduated from there to various off-Broadway stages. She stepped in front of the cameras for the first time in 1977 in a small part in Woody Allen's hugely successful *Annie Hall*. She did one other film, *Madman*, in Israel in 1978, before auditioning for the role of Ripley in *Alien*.

Weaver had no idea how to approach this horror movie set in outer space; it was the furthest thing from her original ambitions. Still, it was a job, and for a struggling New York actor the chance to audition for any film is worth investigating. Ridley Scott's casting of the unknown Weaver was inspired. He dressed the five-foot-ten actor in baggy overalls like the rest of the crew, and she soon reveals herself as tougher than a number of the male characters. But before the audience comes to think of her as just one of the guys, Scott brilliantly inserts a moment where Weaver's femininity and beauty are shown to advantage. In a brief scene before the climactic ending, Ripley seals herself in an escape pod and quickly strips down before donning another, more protective suit. She stands clad in only a skimpy T-shirt and a minute pair of panties before squeezing her exquisitely long legs into the suit. Scott was criticized for being exploitive, but that quick little scene gives the character back her vulnerability and heightens the drama of the movie's final gut-wrenching moments. This was something that sat well with James Cameron when he was resurrecting Ripley in his screenplay. "I tend toward strong female characters anyway — they interest me dramatically."

When Weaver read Cameron's screenplay she was captivated by the storyline that he had created. "The emotional content was much greater this time around." Weaver was relieved. The opening scenes of the movie portray Ripley returning to an entirely different world and being completely haunted by the experiences she endured in her old world. Ripley is no longer an earnest young ensign, but rather a mature officer filled with dread and tormented by loss.

In an early draft of the *Alien* screenplay, Ripley was written as a male character, and Weaver believes that this starting point gives the character much of her force. "It's probably a pretty good idea to do that every once in a while," she says. "That way women can be written as real people without being constantly over-sentimentalized."

Lance Henriksen, too, was keen to work with Cameron again even though he had lost out on *The Terminator* leading role. Henriksen and Cameron are good friends away from the movie sets as well and often get together for dinner. "It was during a Chinese dinner that Jim passed me a copy of his *Aliens* treatment," says Henriksen. "This was not the screenplay, this was just a detailed treatment, and I was completely knocked out by it. That treatment was so well thought out that I swear we could have gone out and shot it as is."

Henriksen was to accept and wonderfully perform the role of the android Bishop, the successor to the android Ash that Ian Holm had played with chilling precision in Ridley Scott's movie. Henriksen wanted to take this character in a different direction, though. Holm had played Ash with pure menace, showing a hint of a smile in only one scene. Henriksen had his own ideas. "I'll put it personally: Bishop is the first time I had a role that I could learn from and really see how far I could take it. I had never had the chance to play an innocent before, and I have that streak in me. I hate the idea of typecasting, and playing Bishop well went a long way to seeing that that wouldn't happen to me."

Henriksen believes that Cameron's fascination with androids and things mechanical is his way of investigating the hero side of his personality. Henriksen connected with this notion. "It was the strangest thing. Even though I was playing an android I felt like it was the most human character I had ever played. I really needed to play that character exactly when I played it, at that exact point in my life."

Aliens was the third movie that Henriksen did with James Cameron and yet Cameron still asked him to audition for the part. Taking nothing for granted, even among friends and proven colleagues, is simply Cameron's way of ensuring that everyone in the cast is there for the right reasons. Sigourney Weaver was, of course, reprising her role from *Alien* and no audition was requested, but even she admitted that she discovered more about Ripley this time around, which can be construed as a tribute to James Cameron's thoughtful writing.

Actor Michael Biehn was another veteran of *The Terminator*, having played Reese in that movie. Biehn is a rugged-looking actor who was born in Alabama and made his way to Los Angeles when he was eighteen. By twenty he had landed a role in the television series *The Runaways*. He had made a few appearances in a handful of low-budget movies before James Cameron tapped him to play Reese. Cameron wanted him for the major role of Hicks, the Marine leader in *Aliens*. Biehn was delighted to be working with Cameron again, but unlike Weaver he was dismayed by the portrayal of his character in the *Aliens* screenplay. He feared that Hicks too closely resembled Reese and immediately went to Cameron with his concerns. The two men worked together to remold the character of Hicks as a likable guy next door.

Biehn openly admits he isn't much of a science fiction buff and that he was quite shocked at how physically demanding making a science fiction epic like *Aliens* was. The weapons that Cameron designed for the space marines were awkwardly heavy, and toting them while running and climbing was a major workout.

James Cameron was a huge fan of the original *Alien* from the moment it was released. He describes his feelings about the film: "I've always been an avid fan of science fiction both in literature and on film. The thing that struck me about *Alien* was the heightened sense of reality — virtually a first for a science fiction film that dealt with a completely separate environment. There were some that were set five years in the future, or whatever, that obviously had a very realistic milieu, but *Alien* was the first film that created an environment with real characters who spoke like real people instead of running around in silver lamé jumpsuits speaking dialogue that is entirely ridiculous."

Cameron was convinced that there was much untapped potential in the character of Ripley. He passionately wanted this sequel to stand on its own and to move in his own direction with it. Because Ripley didn't emerge as the lead character in the original movie until the last third, Cameron had lots of latitude in writing the character for the sequel. "That was one of the things that I found really interesting about the first *Alien* — part of the dramatic focus was intentionally misdirected toward Dallas [Tom Skerritt]. He's the captain of the ship, the guy who is supposed to live, so when he gets killed all bets are off. It was shocking and quite brilliant. *Aliens* features Sigourney Weaver's Ripley from frame one. This prominence provides an opportunity to create a character with more personal and dramatic dimension."

With his background as a graphic artist, Cameron was greatly attracted to *Aliens* by the multitude of designs for vehicles and hardware he would get to play with. He wanted these elements to be up to a standard that would give *Aliens* a distinction that was faithful to but surpassed that of *Alien*.

H. R. Giger, the eccentric Swiss-born artist who designed the original nightmare-inspiring alien for Ridley Scott, was approached about coming on to *Aliens*. Giger wasn't against the idea, but he was committed to another project. Cameron was now faced with a September start date and by May he still had nothing designed. He had to quickly decide whom to bring in to take over and execute the designs that were based on the unique vision that Giger had provided for the first film.

He chose two designers who are among the very best at what they do in the world. Syd Mead was brought in first. Mead is best known for his industrial set designs. He has envisioned and created futuristic landscapes, cityscapes, and vehicles for such movies as *2010*, *Star Trek: The Motion Picture*, and Ridley Scott's landmark futuristic *noir* thriller, *Blade Runner*. Ron Cobb was brought in next. Cobb is one of the most accomplished illustrators and cartoonists ever to work in motion pictures. His designs made a huge impact in *Star Wars*, *Conan the Barbarian*, and *Alien*.

Within three days the pair were already well under way in their task of designing and executing the staggering array of futuristic military vehicles, weapons, and planet-based structures that Cameron was counting on to give the movie exactly the look he envisioned.

Because of the awesome size of the task at hand, Cameron worked out a rigorous and precise shooting schedule. His intention was to shoot the opening sequence first, to give the construction crew more time to prepare the sets. Then panic set in at the production office.

Half Moon Street was shooting across town at the EMI Elstree Studios and it was falling seriously behind schedule. This meant that Sigourney Weaver would be late in arriving at the set. Since she was needed for the opening sequence, Cameron's carefully worked out schedule was now in complete shambles. Only one sequence could be tackled without Weaver — the assault team's move on the atmospheric processing station that has been taken over by the aliens as a nesting area. The sequence involved an elaborate set with a complex hanging miniature, a full-sized armored personnel carrier, high-tech automatic weapons and flame throwers, an alien chest buster (the tiny alien creature that bursts through John Hurt's chest in *Alien*), and a whole swarm of alien creatures. It was the only sequence that needed to be shot not in the studio but in a separate location.

The decision to go outside of the controlled environment of Pinewood Studios was made early on. Cameron either had to build an expensive set at the studio, then overlay it with organic-looking, alien-produced forms, or he could go out and find a structure that he could adapt to his purposes.

Locations manager Peter Lamont and his crew scoured England looking for a deserted gasworks or oil refinery. They finally found a decommissioned electrical generating station in the London suburb of Acton. It was filled with machinery and had grillework floors, making it possible to shoot from one level to another without a lot of complicated setting up after each shot. Cameron loved the location. The grillework allowed light to bleed from one floor to another to create the eerie atmosphere he wanted.

With the immediate scheduling and locations problems solved, *Aliens* was ready to proceed, until a serious safety issue reared its head. The generating plant had been derelict for several years and the asbestos insulation had started to rot, releasing hazardous fibers into the air. A crew had to be brought in to remove all the asbestos before the location could be approved as a safe working environment. Cameron didn't panic; he just had everything done that needed to be done. When a delay is caused by incompetence Cameron can be quick to fly off the handle, but when it is caused by a safety concern he insists that the problem be dealt with properly. Cameron is tough and demanding, but he is known as one of the most safety-conscious directors in the industry.

A key member of the *Aliens* crew was Stan Winston. Winston's fabulous work in *The Terminator* helped make it a global success, and Cameron was quick to sign him up for similar duties on *Aliens*. Winston was delighted. "I loved the first *Alien*," he says. "It is probably my favorite horror movie of the decade, if not of all time. But I have to admit I was a bit disappointed by the ending. When the alien gets blown out into space at the end, you see clearly that it is a guy in a suit. Going into this film I was a bit disheartened by the fact that everyone knew what the alien looked like, so our hands were more or less tied. We had to be true to the original." Cameron responds to those sentiments by saying, "Sure, but being true to the original doesn't necessarily mean enhancing the weaknesses."

With Winston's assistance Cameron was able to capture the aliens on film in a way that made them much more convincing than those in the first film. One ploy was to make the aliens move in a sporadic and furtive manner, like insects. Winston's aliens jump from wall to wall and hang upside down from the ceiling. The alien in the first movie was restricted in its movements because it wore a full-body rubber suit. Cameron and Winston had to come up with a creature that looked similar but was completely different in design. Stan Winston recalls: "What I knew had to be done was to eliminate the rubber suit aspect altogether. After a few kicks at the can I came up with what was essentially a black leotard with carefully placed foam rubber pieces all over it. It was funny because when the leotards were hanging on the rack they looked pretty much like black leotards with little pieces of stuff on them. But on film they were all wet and slimy, and you really can't tell the difference between ours and what was done in the first movie."

It was Cameron's idea to have dancers play the aliens because their greater scope of movement would further the illusion he was trying to achieve. His screenplay had scenes that called for hundreds of aliens to appear at the same time, but he later reduced these to six, then bumped it up to twelve.

Once he had a solid shooting script Cameron agonized

over the approach he would take with the aliens. "In the original *Alien* they went out of their way to cast a very tall person to be inside the suit. The guy they got, Bolaji Bedejo, was actually over seven feet tall," says Cameron. "I knew it would be very hard to find twelve people who were over seven feet tall to play the creatures. So I went back and studied the original movie and found that there was actually only one shot that shows a direct scale relationship between the creature and a human being. I decided that rather than going for height I'd go for people who had the right physiques to be in the suits. Dancers were the thinnest people we could find who also had the strength to do the kinds of movements that we wanted, such as hanging from wires and crawling upside down. They all averaged under six feet, but putting them on footstools or shooting them from low angles made them look menacingly tall."

The aliens themselves were only a small part of the complicated challenges Cameron and his team faced. For the designers, creating a wide array of fantastical vehicles was daunting. In the case of the futuristic armored personnel carrier, Ron Cobb had designed the vehicle with the intention of building it from scratch. Cobb remembers, "I came in with a wedge-shaped design that had kind of a salamander look to it. The thing that I wanted to do most was give it a set of rear wheels that could turn a full 360 degrees so that the vehicle could rotate on its own wheel base. I realized right off the bat that actually building something like that would be on the difficult side, but I thought it was an interesting idea."

Cobb's dilemma illustrates the tension between the ambitions of the film's design team and the reality of its budget and schedule. Building any vehicle from the ground up was cost-prohibitive. A new approach would have to be conceived — and quick.

A solution was found, as it so often is in a James Cameron film, through serendipity. Heathrow Airport in London was replacing two of the tractors that it used to tow jets onto the tarmac, and for a reasonable price it was willing to sell one to the *Aliens* production office. This was just what the designers were looking for, a huge vehicle that could be dressed up to resemble an armored personnel carrier without the worry of whether it could move. When the tractor was delivered to the studio it was discovered that it weighed seventy-two tons: it was armored with thick plate steel and the wheel arches were lined with lead.

Cameron came up with the basic concept of how the vehicle could be altered and draftsman Tony Rimmington came up with a model. They had only three weeks to get the vehicle ready for shooting, and the studio metal shops were already grossly overworked. There was also a concern that the vehicle would simply be too heavy for shooting at the power plant, so the decision was made to keep its use to a bare minimum. The outer layers of steel were peeled away, knocking twenty-eight tons from the total weight.

In the end the vehicle was used in only a couple of shots and its original driver from Heathrow Airport was brought in to drive it. A scale model ended up being used more than anticipated.

All the vehicles were conceived by Cameron, who then turned the ideas over to Syd Mead and Ron Cobb for refinement from an engineering standpoint. Ron Cobb was intrigued by James Cameron; he had never worked with anyone like him before. "When you are working from someone else's designs what you are trying to do is get as close to what you think the originator means as you can," explains Cobb. "That is the way I am accustomed to working. With Jim, he's such an outstanding artist with a very strong visual sense, I'm sure he would design the entire movie himself if he had the time. That made it somewhat hard, because I would have trouble every now and again seeing what Jim wanted me to see. There was nothing wrong with the designs themselves. It was only that I saw them differently than he did."

To hear James Cameron talk about his designs, it becomes evident that he is obsessed with detail. He has a clear view of his idea of perfect and inexactitude simply will not do. "The drop ship" — the vehicle used to transport the troops from the main ship to the ground — "was something I could see very clearly in my mind. I just couldn't seem to draw it. It was like being tongue-tied when you are a public speaker. It defied me. The main problem was not overall configuration, but the variable geometry. Having gun pods fold out and lock down is one example. Finally I decided to go into the studio one day and build a model of it myself. I then turned it over to Ron Cobb and had him take it from there. Specifically, it looked like an Apache AH-64 helicopter, which isn't too surprising since that is what I started from. What I wanted to suggest was an already existing piece of military hardware, then extrapolate beyond that to make it trans-atmospheric, because in space it obviously wouldn't have rotors, but it does have vertical takeoff and landing capability. The motion of it is very helicopter-like, in that the nose dips down when it accelerates and it sort of spins in place when it descends. I wanted my vehicles in the movie to be very specific to helicopter movements."

Perhaps the best-remembered image from *Alien* was the terrifying "face-hugger." We first see this creature when Brett (John Hurt) is investigating the egglike entities on the barren planet LV426. As he leans over one egglike thing, it opens up, revealing a life form encased in a translucent membrane. As he bends closer, something blasts out through the membrane and attaches itself to his face, and a long appendage snakes down his throat.

The face-hugger designed by H. R. Giger was to play a significant role in *Aliens*, but the design team decided to take a second look at what they were working with. Stan Winston hesitantly made some changes. "We took a few artistic liberties but nothing too drastic or even notice-able. We made the knuckles look a bit more knuckle-like and we lengthened the tail by about six inches so we could do more with it."

As always, Cameron's rethinking of the original *Alien* led to designs that were more difficult to execute. That is what makes his movies so fascinating to watch: the images are so fantastic that we don't have time to take a breath and say, "I wonder how he did that." In *Alien* the face-hugger could be positioned but its joints were unarticulated. The face-huggers for *Aliens* required a full range of motion, and the script demanded that several variations of the creature be developed. In some scenes the face-huggers are dead and sealed in tubes; in others they are horrifyingly alive. In one sequence the face-hugger that attaches itself to Sigourney Weaver is a fully articulated cable-controlled puppet. And then there were the shots where face-huggers had to scuttle across the floor convincingly. Stan Winston found that these little gadgets were the ones that required the most thought. "I wanted to do a pull-toy type of thing where we would literally pull it across the floor and a wheel would turn underneath it or something, and that would cause the legs to move. In a way that was pretty much exactly what we ended up doing. But when we were just starting out we really couldn't figure out how we were going to realize that one."

One of the ideas that Cameron had was to put a small

high-torque motor or a model airplane engine inside the face-huggers, but Stan Winston couldn't find a way to make this work. The solution proved to be a simple one that Cameron had used before.

Late one night Cameron called Stan Winston at his design studio in California and excitedly described to him what he had done with his rubber fish in *Piranha 2*. He described a fish being pulled through the water with wires that were rigged up with a little mechanism that caused the tail to wiggle as it was being pulled along. The next day Winston set about applying that technique to one of the rubber face-huggers. He installed a gear mechanism that wiggled the little legs when the creature was pulled along the floor. The faster you pulled the wire, the faster the little legs would move.

One of the most eccentric, dazzling ideas that Cameron came up with on *Aliens* was the power loader. This was a kind of wearable forklift with moveable arms and legs that the operator worked from inside the machine. A joy stick controlled a pair of eight-foot-long lifting arms and a ser-vomechanism allowed movement of its squat hydraulic legs. As strange as this piece of equipment looked, it *appeared* quite convincingly practical. Like everything having to do with the movie, Cameron had fully thought this contrap-tion through. "I suppose it would be theoretically possible to build such a piece of equipment but I don't think it would be practical in any other environment other than in zero gravity where the power loader could have electric cleats on its feet."

Cameron could dream and sketch all he wanted, but the construction of the power loader was the responsibility of designer John Richardson. Richardson describes the assignment. "I was asked to design and build this thing — which is not the kind of thing you are asked to build every day. It was June and I had to deliver a working power loader to the set by October. I was really worried that we wouldn't make our date because the design phase was taking so long. Most directors would simply say, 'I want you to design a walking forklift kind of thing.' Jim Cameron says he wants you to design and build a walking forklift but he wants the bolts to be shaped this way and the rivets to be visible here. He is very pedantic about the fine details and very particular about the overall aesthetic. But from my point of view, it just didn't have to look a certain way, it also had to do a bunch of things." Cameron recalls with a smile, "John Richardson and I absolutely hated each other for months. Then when it looked like it was all going to finally come together, we started to get enthusiastic again."

Cameron's idea that the aliens be governed by a horrific alien queen proved to be both the movie's biggest challenge and what made it so memorable. From the start Cameron wanted this alien monarch to be as tall as fourteen feet.

His original sketches were starkly beautiful renditions of a huge creature that looked like a cross between a *Tyrannosaurus rex* and a praying mantis. Cameron's designs were at the same time original and logical extrapolations of what Giger had designed for the first film. He is proud of what he came up with. "Even though Giger was not directly involved in the project, his ghost was hanging over us constantly," says Cameron. "I must say, though, that I feel a sense of authorship over this queen. Someone once described her as an anorexic dinosaur, which I suppose is inevitable, but is not quite what I had in mind, at least not overtly, because that would have been far too common-place and boring. For me, the queen is really a blend of what Giger does with what I wanted to do, which was to create something big and powerful and terrifying and fast and female. Hideous and beautiful at the same time, like a black widow spider."

Stan Winston was assigned to execute Cameron's plans for the fantastic alien queen. Cameron presented his sketches to Winston along with his ideas on how the model of the queen might be rendered on screen as a full-sized artifact. Winston was immediately attracted to the design but more than a little daunted by the prospect of building such a large-scale mechanical creature that could function convincingly without a stuntman inside — not to mention the difficulty in trying to conceal all the support mechanisms and all the external activators. Still, Winston was intrigued by the proposition and he knew better than to tell James Cameron that it probably couldn't be done.

Winston altered Cameron's designs, losing a few arms here and changing the joint structure of the legs there. After months of long and complex work, the alien queen was built and ready to put into action. Initially, all went well with the fourteen-foot-high queen and with the smaller model versions. Then came time for the climactic battle between Ripley in the power loader and the alien queen. The principal photography schedule was coming rapidly to an end, even though the effects team was looking at another four solid months of work. Added to the time pressures was the tension brewing between Cameron and the effects company he had hired, L.A. Effects Group.

Cameron had written and orchestrated a wild brawl between Ripley and the alien queen that goes on for fifteen minutes and ends with both of them tumbling into an open air lock. The effects team, especially designer John Richardson, were more concerned about this sequence than anything else in the movie. Richardson explains, "There was a lot of stuff happening in the sequence all at once. The alien queen was moving around all over the place doing a series of complex movements and the power loader was doing what it does. The set was just filled with all kinds of effects people pulling wires and working levers. It was quite a sight. My concern, though, was the power loader's ability to take all the banging around it was going to have to take. This thing was constructed out of vacuformed plastic."

Cameron was also anxious about the sequence. He had written it, as he writes most of his sequences, in a flurry of inspiration, but a real person was going to have to act out his imaginings. "My main concern was for Sigourney Weaver," Cameron explains. "I had hired special effects guys who I knew could do the job, so I was confident that everything would happen, but in the case of the battle between the alien queen and Ripley I knew there was going to be a lot of fits and starts and a lot of takes. But in the end she was just wonderful about the whole thing. She was a complete pro and very tolerant when it came to standing around the set for hours doing the predicted take after take."

Early in the production James Cameron and Gale Anne Hurd met with British visual effects wizard Brian Johnson to see if he might be interested in acting as the overall purveyor of the visual effects. Johnson had won two Academy Awards for his visual effects for *Alien* and *The Empire Strikes Back*. He was intrigued, but then he heard that Cameron and Hurd had decided to hire L.A. Effects Group. Johnson assumed that he'd heard the last of the situation.

L.A. Effects went to work developing the motion-control effects that Cameron needed. It quickly became obvious that they had bitten off more than they could chew. The systems they had shipped to Pinewood Studios in England proved to be woefully inadequate for the job.

Cameron wasted no time looking around for someone else. There were few motion-control effects specialists in England. One of the best firms was an outfit called Arkadon Motion Control, founded by Brian Johnson with Dennis Lowe and Nick Pollack. Cameron called Johnson, who was on vacation in the Caribbean, and Johnson returned immediately to England to take over. The crew had to work fast and furious to achieve the effects in the allotted time. Johnson delivered the last of his special effects shots in early May. Six weeks later the movie was finished and four weeks later it opened in movie theaters to full houses but mixed critical response.

Variety said the film was "a very worthy follow-up to Ridley Scott's 1979 sci-fi shocker" and described Sigourney Weaver as doing "a smashing job here as Ripley, one of the great female screen roles of recent years. The strength with which she invests the part is invigorating, and the actress really gets down and dirty with tremendous flair." Cameron, however, was not as roundly praised. "Although the film accomplishes everything it aims to do, Cameron suffers just a bit by comparison to Ridley Scott in that his eye for visuals isn't nearly as fine. The overall impression is of a film made by an expert craftsman, while Scott clearly has something of an artist in him." The *New York Times* was even less generous, calling the sequel "a touch less innovative than its predecessor" in a review that was largely dismissive of the movie.

Aliens went on to earn a surprising (given that it was a sci-fi/horror movie) seven Academy Award nominations, including ones for art direction and visual effects.

Aliens marked the first foray into big-budget movie-making for both James Cameron and Gale Anne Hurd, but they remained committed to a no-frills approach to film-making. Both are completely obsessed with getting virtually every cent up on the screen. *Aliens* cost a relatively cheap $18 million and was a huge hit, earning more than $80 million. Gale Anne Hurd clarifies their strategy: "The approach that we have to filmmaking — even with a larger budget like this one — is bare bones. Instead of doing the typical things you would expect on a big-budget movie, we made this like we were down to our last dollar every day. We employed people we had worked with at New World, we went right to Stan Winston for the effects because we'd worked with him before. We also had the advantage of Jim's background in special effects that really helped us do all our troubleshooting in advance. He knew what he was looking for." In spite of his reputation and subsequent breaking of the record for most expensive movie three times (first with *Terminator 2: Judgment Day*, then with *True Lies* and *Titanic*), Cameron is simply not a profligate spender. *Aliens* came in on time and on budget and Cameron proved he could make an expensive studio movie responsibly.

"It's not that we didn't have enough money, it's almost that we didn't want the money," he explains. "I know nobody will believe that, but it's true. People tend to use the size of a budget as a yardstick for how good a movie is, but I think a lot of recent productions have really killed the viability of the science fiction film because the people making them have believed that throwing enormous amounts of money at them will get the job done. And it doesn't work that way. For one thing it is diminishing the returns beyond a certain point — the extra money just allows a certain polish, it's just putting a higher buff on something you already had. And sometimes a shot that cost twice as much to get isn't twice as good. The first thing you learn as a director is that you can't get it perfect on the set. The place to make it perfect is in the editing room or on the dubbing stage. If the characters are good and the story works, then the audience will go with it. If the story doesn't work, then the best, most elaborate special effects ever achieved aren't going to keep them in their seats."

Cameron's achievement in *Aliens* is astounding. He took an established classic and made an altogether satisfying sequel that out-grossed and out-thrilled the original but remained true to its spirit. The third installment, *Alien 3* (1992), directed by David Fincher, tried to return to the gothic origins of Ridley Scott's film, and it showed just what an error in judgment trying to recapture that feeling would have been for Cameron.

The success of *Aliens* put Cameron in a great position. He was now an A-list filmmaker. He was happily married to his business partner and he was awash with ideas about what to do next. He decided to embark on a cinematic adventure that is still described as the toughest movie shoot in history. James Cameron was about to go from the highest of highs into *The Abyss*.

Seven

SPLASHDOWN: THE MAKING OF *THE ABYSS*

"When you look long into an abyss, the abyss also looks into you."

FRIEDRICH NIETZSCHE

The period between the success of *Aliens* and the decision to go ahead and make *The Abyss* was fairly short. Cameron found himself in the position of being able to pick and choose what he would do next, and rather than doing the project with the highest profile or the biggest fee he chose to do what all good writers and directors want to do, something of his own.

Twentieth Century Fox was delighted with the box-office performance of *Aliens*, especially since another expensive film, John Carpenter's *Big Trouble in Little China*, had failed to live up to expectations earlier in the summer of 1986. They were only too happy to work again with James Cameron, the new hit-maker. Fox executives were intrigued with the idea behind *The Abyss* but they knew it was potentially problematic. This one had logistical difficulty written all over it. But James Cameron's enthusiasm and his cool reassured Fox, and they gave him the green light.

The Abyss was born in Cameron's adolescent daydreams in a high-school biology class in 1970. Back then, James Cameron was a scrawny, pimply-faced teenager uncomfortable in his own skin, not to mention the rigid social structure of high school. He often took to drawing elaborate comic-book panels in the backs of his textbooks to ward off abject boredom. During one biology class he absent-mindedly started writing a short story called "The Abyss," which was part fantasy and part trolling of his own nightmares and dreamscapes. The inspiration for the story came on a class trip to a science exhibition in Buffalo. Cameron listened in stunned wonderment as a lecturer described the experience of breathing liquid oxygen. This started the wheels of his imagination turning. "The Abyss" ultimately became the spine of the $50-million epic movie he was to make eighteen years later. A lot was added to that original story, but the fundamental concept was unchanged.

The high-school short fiction effort concerned a race of aliens who have been inhabiting the uncharted depths of our oceans since before man evolved on earth and can manipulate water for their own purposes. These aliens become concerned about the pattern of self-destruction they are detecting from the surface of the earth and fear that their environment, which heretofore has been peaceful, might be threatened by petty earthly squabbles.

The short story is a cautionary tale about a more advanced race of beings threatening the virtual destruction of mankind to preserve their own safety, thus forcing humans to resolve their differences collectively in the face of a much larger threat. Hardly an original premise, but Cameron did manage to give it his own spin. His aliens don't come down from above; they were on Earth before we were. Cameron remembers, "To say that when I was sitting in biology class writing that story that I was thinking to myself, twenty years from now I'm going to take this story and make a $50-million movie out of it, would be a bit on the revisionist side. But on the other hand, I waste nothing. I'm like the Plains Indians, who would kill a buffalo for the meat but would then use every other part for some practical purpose or another. I can say quite honestly, though, that I tinkered with the story of *The Abyss* that I wrote in biology class when I was seventeen from the day I wrote it until the day the special edition laser disc was released."

8

An American submarine carrying Trident missiles sinks to the bottom of the sea after being accosted by some unknown creature that passed them at an unnaturally fast speed. The Navy organizes a rescue mission to be carried out by a team of highly trained Navy SEALs, but since the sub is resting on a plateau at a great depth they will need help from an experimental deep-sea oil-drilling rig, *Deepcore*, that is anchored nearby.

Bud Brigman (Ed Harris) is the foreman aboard *Deepcore* and he receives the news of their enlistment into this rescue operation with great skepticism, saying that his crew are oil workers, not a rescue team. The Navy steps in and explains that this is a matter of national security and that a rescue team will soon be on the way down to carry out the mission.

When the SEALs arrive they are accompanied by the designer of *Deepcore*, who is described as "the queen bitch of the universe." She is also Bud's ex-wife, Lindsay Brigman (Mary Elizabeth Mastrantonio). To make matters a bit more dicey, a major tropical storm is heading their way.

Bud, while being wary of these "Navy jarheads," follows instructions and starts to move *Deepcore* to the submarine's location. The SEALs are tough guys and certainly lacking in the sense of humor department. The leader, Lieutenant Coffey (Michael Biehn), is the toughest of them all, but he is starting to show signs of high-pressure nervous disorder. Bud and his men are asked to help the SEALs as a diving support team. As the SEAL team makes its way down to the disabled submarine it becomes quite clear that they are not going to rescue people; they are more interested in securing the code book needed to launch the Trident missiles. Once inside the sub, one of Bud's crew sees a bright, luminescent "something" that he deliriously calls an angel.

Lindsay is hovering above the sub in a submersible when she sees a similarly luminescent fast-moving craft that approaches her, considers her, then takes off through the water at an enormous speed.

Coffey takes these reports to his superiors, describing the encounters as being with possible Soviet aggressors. He is given permission to return to the sub, arm one of the warheads, and wait for further instructions.

Hurricane Frederick is lashing the *Explorer, Deepcore's* surface support vessel. High winds blow a huge steel crane off the deck and it sinks straight down to the unsuspecting *Deepcore.* The crane narrowly misses *Deepcore* but then slips down into a deep trough, threatening to take *Deepcore* over the edge with it. The *Deepcore* rig is dragged along the ocean floor, causing extensive damage and costing the lives of a few crew members. The result is that all communication with the world above is cut off, and the people aboard *Deepcore* are running out of air.

Lindsay ventures out in diving gear to assess the damage to her beloved rig. She is approached by a dazzling pink creature. This visitor is followed by a large glowing craft that rises up from the depths of the trough. Lindsay tries to make contact but the creature quickly disappears back into the depths.

Aboard *Deepcore* Lindsay describes her experiences to the amazed crew. Coffey, now firmly in the throes of a serious case of psychosis and dangerously paranoid, locks all nonmilitary people away in one section of the rig so that he and his men can go about doing what needs to be done without interference.

What follows is the most visually spectacular alien visitation sequence ever put on film. An alien intelligence visits *Deepcore* in the form of a long tentacle of sea water that snakes its way through the passageways and compartments of the vessel, imitating in watery form whomever it encounters. It makes its way into the area where the oil workers are imprisoned, then snakes through to the compartment where the warhead is being kept. Coffey panics when he sees it. He straps the warhead onto a submersible that is programmed to go into the trough to photograph whatever is down there. The warhead is set to detonate in three hours.

Bud escapes and engages Coffey in a fight. Just when Bud figures he's beaten Coffey, Coffey jumps into the armed submersible and disappears into the water. Bud dons scuba gear and gives chase. Lindsay gets into another submersible to assist Bud. A wild undersea submersible-against-submersible fight takes place during which Coffey is killed.

But his armed submersible slips into the trough and continues on as programmed.

Bud quickly suits up in a deep-sea diving suit and allows himself to be lowered into the trough to try to disarm the warhead. As he sinks to depths never before visited by man (in a suit that requires him to breathe liquid oxygen), signs of a pressure-induced nervous disorder kick in.

Bud arrives at the warhead confused and disoriented. He manages to defuse the bomb and then resigns himself to his fate. He hasn't enough air left to return to the surface. But he is suddenly rescued by an angelic-looking alien who takes him to an undersea city, where he is shown images of violence and destruction, of man's inhumanity to man down through history. The last image that the aliens show Bud is of the final computer message Bud sent Lindsay from the depths of the trough. It says simply, "I love you wife" — the implication being that Bud's self-sacrifice was what convinced the aliens that human beings were capable of redemption.

The storm on the surface clears. The crew of *Deepcore* reports that they are running out of air and have lost several members, including Bud. Bud then responds with a message using a portable computer attached to his wrist: "Have some new friends down here ..."

The huge alien ship, opalescent like the inside of a conch shell, rises up, bringing not only Bud back to the surface but the disabled *Deepcore* as well.

8

The Abyss was released by Twentieth Century Fox in August 1989. It had been scheduled for earlier in the summer, but the complexity of the post-production special visual effects work delayed the release. The film is still considered the most physically difficult movie shoot in the history of movie production. Problems on *The Abyss* were a day-to-day event, some entirely unforeseeable, some easily predictable given the nature of the story that Cameron was setting out to tell. And some problems can be placed firmly on the shoulders of James Cameron, whose reputation for perfectionism and obstinacy was not unjustified.

As often happens in Hollywood when a red-hot director sets his sights on an idea for his next project, the lesser talents in town scramble to put similarly themed knock-off projects into development to pre-empt the big talent. Generally speaking, these knock-offs are easier to get off the ground and far less time-consuming to produce. Cameron fell victim to this syndrome during the making of *The Abyss*. After *Aliens* had moved him to the top of the A-list in Hollywood, an announcement was made that Cameron, Gale Anne Hurd, and Twentieth Century Fox would team up on a project about alien life forms. But this time the film would be set not in outer space but in the depths of the unexplored sea bottom.

The stage was quickly set for Cameron's low-budget competitors, who realized that his impossibly difficult project would be a long time in production, to rush their own undersea alien horror movies to the screen. First out of the gate was *Deepstar Six*, from director Sean Cunningham, who had made *Friday the 13th* in 1980, about a sea monster that attacks an ocean-bottom research team that is trying to create a deep-sea launching site for Navy missiles. *Deepstar Six* had a cast of mostly TV series actors and it didn't make even the tiniest splash at the box office.

Next up was *Leviathan*, directed by *Rambo* director George Pan Cosmatos. It was shot in Italy and written by David Peoples, who was responsible for the excellent *Blade Runner* (1982) and Clint Eastwood's multi-Oscar *Unforgiven* (1992). *Leviathan* featured an interesting cast that included Peter Weller and Richard Crenna, and a story about a mining camp on the floor of the Atlantic Ocean. The crew are attacked by gruesome creatures after one member brings something back with him from the wreckage of a Russian cargo ship. MGM backed *Leviathan* with some major promotion, but again there was no audience for this undersea action/horror yarn.

Twentieth Century Fox was concerned about the failure of the these two similarly themed movies, but they were confident that James Cameron and Gale Anne Hurd could blow both of them out of the water. Hurd remembers the spot they found themselves in. "Making *The Abyss* was really an all-or-nothing proposition. Once we put this huge, gargantuan machine in motion we either had to go with it right on down the line or watch it collapse around us. But I knew we were really onto something here. I knew that Jim could be making one of the most visually dazzling, exciting movies ever made. We knew it was going to be tough going in, we just had no idea how tough."

What has to be remembered in any discussion of the making of *The Abyss* is the difference between intentionally difficult and reckless. No one was more aware of this distinction than James Cameron. "What we were doing was unique," he says, "in that the normal rules of filmmaking didn't really apply, but the same results needed to be achieved. We were under water a great deal of the time and safety was a big issue, but we also needed to do what needed to get done. The nature of the risks we were taking and the environment we were in had to be respected at all times."

By the time *The Abyss* was ready to go into active pre-production Cameron and Hurd's marriage was starting to collapse under the great weight of the tension the couple was feeling after working so closely together for so long. The size of this project dictated that a strictly professional demeanor be maintained throughout the making of the picture. They both knew a lot of eyes were on them and that any sign of trouble might cause nervous fingers at the studio to reach for the plug.

The couple tried hard not to allow their off-screen tensions to bleed over into the production, but the lines often became blurred, causing dual camps of supporters to form. The making of a movie always brings together a strange, tightly knit community with very little contact with the outside world, and personal squabbles are often magnified out of proportion. Add the marital tensions to the fact that the studio gave Hurd and Cameron only four months in which to shoot the movie and it made for a highly combustible set. "Everyone really rose to the challenge on this one," says Cameron. "No one ever said, 'I can't do that.' I'm very proud of the people who went through this with me. I hope they are all proud of themselves as well. We made this enormously difficult picture and we did it with a minimum of compromise."

Cameron and Hurd were criticized when the movie got into trouble for possibly underplaying the difficulty of the underwater shooting that would be required. Since nothing this big and complex had ever been attempted, there would be no way to underplay or overplay what might be awaiting them. Cameron freely admits that his enthusiasm carried him a fair distance. "I just assumed that I could infect everyone around me with my enthusiasm. People were going out of their way to tell me how crazy I was, but I kept telling them that sure, it looks impossible on the surface, but we still have to do it."

Once the backing of Twentieth Century Fox was firmly in place, the decision of where to shoot the movie had to be made. The available sets ideal for underwater shooting

all proved to be woefully inadequate. The largest underwater movie set was in Malta, but it was deemed inacces-
sible for the crew and the tons of equipment that would be
used. It was time for Cameron to get creative. "I toyed
with the idea of constructing an underwater soundstage of
sorts, but then the specs and the costs came in and they
were ridiculously high. Plan B had to be devised and it had
to be devised quickly."

Plan B turned out to be a stroke of pure genius. Cameron
stumbled across some information that immediately set
bells ringing. In Gaffney, South Carolina, he found the disused and unfinished Cherokee Nuclear Energy Plant. It
had already been bought by a low-budget filmmaker named
Earl Owensby, but Owensby didn't have the resources to
do anything with it. Cameron assembled a survey team and
headed with Hurd to the site. It was perfect. Daunting, but
perfect. Cameron took his good luck as a positive omen.

Work at the Cherokee plant commenced the instant
the paperwork was completed. The huge silo was flooded
with 10 million gallons of water after sets, some weighing
as much as forty tons each, were assembled. A special fil-
tration system had to be devised to keep the water as clear
as possible at all times. The size and complexity of this set
would be a constant source of frustration.

James Cameron was so anxious about the possibility of being
undercut by knock-off artists that he would allow actors

reading for the smaller parts in *The Abyss* to look at the screenplay only in his presence. Actors being considered for leading roles and craftsmen being interviewed for positions on the movie were given numbered copies of the screenplay that they were to read straight through, then return. Nondisclosure agreements were drawn up for cast and crew to sign that promised dismissal if a copy of the screenplay bearing their assigned number turned up anywhere other than in their possession.

Cameron's screenplay for *The Abyss* is an engrossing read. The descriptions are vivid and specific. Ed Harris remembers the first time he read *The Abyss*. "I immediately got what Jim was trying to do when I read this screenplay. This was a balls-out action/adventure film, but it was one that had a soul. I was completely into it right away."

The cast that Hurd and Cameron assembled was a mixture of familiar faces and complete unknowns. Early on in the development stages Cameron decided not to use big-name, above-the-title stars, preferring to concentrate on casting solid actors who were willing to toil away for months in a moviemaking environment of unprecedented hardship.

"The studio suggested that I cast a very big name in the lead role," remembers Cameron, "but I resisted. I had my own notion of what people should represent in the movie, but they were really adamant. Then I put it to a dollars and cents equation and that got their attention. Casting the actor they were suggesting would have added between $6 and $8 million to the budget. I ended up getting exactly who I wanted in this film. I'm usually pretty lucky that way."

Solid character actor Ed Harris was cast as the tool-pusher Bud Brigman. Harris had first received critical praise and an Academy Award nomination for playing *Mercury* astronaut John Glenn in Philip Kaufman's brilliant *The Right Stuff* (1983), but he had failed to parlay that boost into a leading-man career. When presented with the chance to star in a gigantic summer adventure movie — a James Cameron movie — Harris saw an opportunity he couldn't pass up. By the end of this production it would be a decision that he would rethink a hundred times. Harris comments: "I remember going into this thinking that stunt divers would cover off anything that might be too dangerous or might be done more efficiently, because stunt divers actually know what they are doing. I had no idea going in that I would be doing the kind of things in this movie that I ended up doing."

Michael Biehn also jumped at the chance to be in *The Abyss*. "Working with Jim Cameron provides an actor with the opportunity not only to do quality work but to live out an adventure," he enthuses. "Although I have to admit, I really couldn't have imagined just how much of an adventure this one would end up being."

For his female lead, Lindsay Brigman, the tough oil-rig design engineer, it was imperative that Cameron cast someone who could project both an alluring sensuality and a tough-as-nails attitude at the same time. After being turned down by a few actors, he connected with the tall, feisty Italian-American Mary Elizabeth Mastrantonio. Mastrantonio had made a major impression as the ill-fated sister of Al Pacino's Tony Montana in her film debut in Brian DePalma's crime epic *Scarface* (1983). She subsequently appeared in several major motion pictures, including Martin Scorsese's sequel to the 1961 classic *The Hustler, The Color of Money,* and the Kevin Costner film *Robin Hood: Prince of Thieves.* Like Ed Harris, Mastrantonio could not resist the female lead in such a big, intriguing movie. She explains the allure of *The Abyss:* "I was interested in the character of Lindsay, but I was also interested in the adventure that this one was promising. I remember being hugely impressed by Jim Cameron when I met him. This man was completely focused and could describe and defend all of his ideas with clarity and enthusiasm. Before it was over I'd want to kill him at least a dozen times."

Once the cast was assembled and the sets were built, it became obvious that much of what needed to be done by the actors was dangerous. All involved were enthusiastic enough, but there are laws governing the amount of danger actors and crew members are to be exposed to. James Cameron was in a difficult spot. "The problem I was having with taking the cast into the water was the survival of the script. When submerged that deep and in all that gear and when you aren't all that experienced [with diving], it is hard to get the basic survival instinct out of the way and stay focused on the dramatic requirements of the shot you are trying to do."

To guarantee the safety of the cast and crew, everyone was put through a rigorous training program. Professional divers were brought in to teach the advanced diver training that is usually reserved for diving instructors.

While the cast and crew were getting up to speed, James Cameron was also having to deal with a far more pressing set of logistical problems. Cameron's screenplay sets much of the action deep in an ocean trough where no natural light penetrates. Cameron had to somehow block the light that was filtering down to his sets from the surface of the vast tank. He tried out various materials to cover the tank, but they were too costly or unreliable. Finally he settled on a layer of buoyant plastic beads that floated on the water.

Cameron's unwavering confidence was his greatest strength: "It was just one thing after another. But the enormity of this undertaking never discouraged me. If anything it encouraged me." In short order the cast and crew started feeling the pressure. Ed Harris remarked in the early days of the production, "I'm starting to have problems with the physical requirements of this movie."

Mike Cameron, James's younger brother, was brought in to help work out some technicals, including the serious issue of underwater camera movement. Mike is an aeronautical engineer and a born inventor. Early tests indicated that the shots using the underwater rigged cameras looked uneven and wobbly. The Brothers Cameron put their heads together and came up with something they called the Sea Wasp. This was a small underwater camera operated by a motor that provided smoother motion through the water. The Sea Wasp was the first of five cinematic equipment patents that the brothers would earn during the course of shooting *The Abyss.*

Cameron also insisted that a better method of replenishing the actors' air supplies was needed, as repeatedly resurfacing would be too time-consuming. He devised a kind of underwater filling station that would allow everyone to fill their tanks while remaining submerged.

The face-obscuring helmet and mask rig the actors wore provided more difficulties, but they too were solved to everyone's satisfaction by the development of a full-face mask that allowed the camera to see the entire face of the actor inside from several angles. The helmet also had a built-in communications system that enabled Cameron to speak to his cast and crew under water. "The helmets were really something. They allowed me to speak to everyone but they couldn't speak back to me. It was a director's dream, really," laughs Cameron. (Cameron was so happy with this new self-developed apparatus that he conducted filmed interviews for a "making of *The Abyss*" documentary under water in full gear.) Because this helmet had no track record, several elaborate safety drills were devised to get everyone comfortably familiar with its feel and function.

Even with this constant regard for the safety of everyone involved there was still tension. Cameron and Ed Harris had a running battle throughout the shoot. Harris repeatedly asked himself if making this movie was worth risking his life. Harris describes part of his frustration this way: "We'd have this big board set up where we'd map out everything — where everyone was going to be and how everything was going to unfold. But it's real easy to say what you're going to do on land. Once you get down there in forty feet of water, all of a sudden things don't work out quite the same way."

In one sequence Harris and the burly actor Leo Burmester must swim forty or more feet under water from one pod to another without the benefit of scuba gear. Safety divers were close by with supplies of air should anything go wrong, but that provided only small comfort to the actors. After two or three grueling takes Harris and Burmester were frustrated and exhausted. A few more takes were required before the proper amount of coverage was obtained. Only Cameron's passion and utter dedication kept the actors from mutinying. Cameron was right there in the water for hour upon hour with them; he was not asking anyone to do anything that he wasn't either doing or willing to do himself. Ed Harris recalls: "I have a scene with Michael [Biehn] where we are having a knock-down, drag-out fist fight while in about a foot and a half of water in a submersible docking area. The fight was quite physical and the terrain on the set was a bit on the challenging side, filled with pipes and irregular-shaped hatchways. And the water was fucking cold. At the end of this scene I was completely exhausted and frustrated past the point I have ever been before."

Harris describes occasions when he was being driven back to his hotel after a day's shooting so physically drained that he broke down in wracking sobs. Then the next day he got up and did it all over again.

Mary Elizabeth Mastrantonio recalls that "it took hours to set up even the most straightforward of shots — it really boggled my mind the level of patience and dedication to vision that Jim had. Watching the movie, you really have no idea just how difficult each sequence was to get on film. The scene during which I first encounter the aliens under water had me just looking straight ahead with a look of wonder on my face. I was actually looking off in the distance at a stunt diver who was floating out of camera range. This simple shot took us all day to get."

Needing to have all of his shots intricately worked out in advance, Cameron relied, out of sheer necessity, on storyboards on *The Abyss*. Because the phrase "time is money" is never more true than on a movie set, Cameron and Hurd had to draw up a realistic schedule that would take into account both the budget and the fact that with this much underwater shooting they could only guess at how long the movie would take to shoot.

Cameron had used ace effects man Stan Winston on most of his movies to date, so when Steve Johnson was hired to design the effects for *The Abyss* the rumors started to fly. One often repeated story, which Johnson himself disavows, had it that Winston was contacted first but he said the words that do not exist in James Cameron's vocabulary: "It's impossible" and "It can't be done." The truth is that Winston was contractually tied up on another film.

Steve Johnson is a talkative, intelligent, immensely talented guy who shares the view held by a lot of people who have worked for James Cameron: it is the toughest thing he has ever had to do and he would do it again in a minute. "One thing I picked up working for Jim was that everyone around him, even the most experienced, talented people, actively sought his approval and tried to gain his praise," states Johnson, who rates his own work on *The Abyss* as the best he's ever done.

Johnson was so infected by Cameron's wide-eyed descriptions of what he was going to put on the screen that he disregarded the inner voice telling him that a lot of what he was being asked to do was seemingly impossible. Johnson recalls, "When I first read the script I remember thinking that these were effects that, as written, simply could not be achieved. The demands of this project were absolutely devastating. But Jim inspired me to my very depths. I left our first meeting thinking: I'll make this happen!"

A lot was riding on the shoulders of Johnson and his crew. If the aliens in this movie weren't eye-poppingly unique, then all the efforts of building the underwater sets would be drastically diminished. Working from Cameron's designs and a few early designs from the renowned comic-book artist Moebius, whose talents Cameron had enlisted to give the designs the kind of distinctive feel that Giger had given *Alien*, Johnson and his crew went to work

Johnson remembers, "The basic problem I had was three-pronged. I was asked to create a creature that would work under water, that was glass clear, and was self-illuminating. The problem was when we got the creature ready that would work under water it wasn't transparent. When we got one that was glass clear, it wasn't self-illuminating. When we got a creature that was glass clear and self-illuminating, the fucking thing wouldn't work under water."

Johnson rose to every challenge Cameron posed, designing physical solutions. In Johnson's opinion *The Abyss* is probably the last movie of this kind to be done that way; soon afterwards computer-generated images began to dominate moviemaking.

One story that Johnson tells is indicative of Cameron's capacity to inspire fear — and affectionate respect — on the set. "We were shooting group shots of aliens in a Plexiglas tank that held about 200,000 gallons of water. We were testing puppets as they swooped around the tank. I was very concerned about failures and breakdowns, so I didn't want too much swooping going on. We start rehearsing and I look into the tank and I see all these puppets swooping around — exactly the opposite of what I had requested. So I rush up the ladder and yell at the crew, 'I told you to cool it during rehearsal and save the fucking things for the shoot!' They turn to me and say, 'Mr. Cameron told us that he wanted to see the things in motion.' I cut them off by yelling, 'I don't give a fuck what he said, I'm telling you to cool it until the actual take.'

"Well, just by the looks on their faces I knew that I was dead. I turned around and Jim Cameron was standing right behind me. I couldn't do anything but give him this big goofball smile. I was expecting the absolute worst, but Jim was actually very cool about it. He asked me to explain the statement, so I did. I tried to make my point of view sound as urgent as possible. He looked at me with one of those off-in-the-distance, thoughtful looks of his and said, 'You're probably right.'

"I heaved a sigh of relief, but not because I was worried about him yelling at me or berating me in front of the crew, but because I wanted his approval. Everyone wanted his approval."

By this time Cameron and Hurd were all but estranged, and the stress was showing more so on Hurd than on Cameron.

Hurd decided to staff the production office and be on the set only when absolutely required. Cameron reflects, "I can't really say what it was that drove a wedge between Gale and me but once it was there, it was there. I have always been attracted to women that did not really need me at all." Cameron's personal life since he started making films has revolved around his work, and *The Abyss* was certainly no exception.

Shooting proceeded with Cameron firmly in control. Fox were impressed by Cameron's confidence and were stunned by the sensational footage they were seeing. "Once shooting started, I had no intention of shooting a foot of film until all the logistics were worked out completely to my satisfaction," states Cameron. "The studio was applying pressure on us to finish the movie quickly, but I had to stay focused and clear-headed. *The Abyss* had to be the movie that I set out to make. It's funny, but it quickly became very clear to me that no matter how impossible it seemed on the surface, that not only could this be done but we could push the envelope further than it had ever been pushed before. That was a powerfully exhilarating feeling."

Industrial Light & Magic is the trailblazing special effects company that George Lucas founded in 1975 as he was gearing up to make his landmark movie *Star Wars*. It was headed by master effects craftsman John Dykstra. They set up shop in an old warehouse in Van Nuys, California, and grew rapidly in direct proportion to the growth of their burgeoning reputation as the premiere effects house in the world. Lucas relocated ILM to San Raphael, California, to do the myriad of effects required for his *Star Wars* sequel *The Empire Strikes Back*. ILM is a division of LucasFilm Ltd. and has created the effects for such blockbusters as the *Star Trek* movies, *ET: The Extraterrestrial, Back to the Future,* and *Jurassic Park*. ILM was brought in to augment the work that Steve Johnson was doing and add other visual effects, the likes of which had never been tried before. Included in the ILM mandate were several scenes involving the alien shape-shifter made out of sea water. When this snaking water alien confronts Harris and Mastrantonio, it molds itself into accurate representations of their faces. ILM's computer-generated images used in this scene were at the cutting edge for their time.

Back in Gaffney at the Cherokee plant, stories were filtering out about heated arguments and cast and crew being verbally abused by the demanding Cameron. It was alleged that Cameron was working the cast and crew to the point of physical collapse and humiliating crew members who made mistakes via a large bank of speakers that allowed the entire production team to hear the dressing-down loud and clear. Fox executives were growing concerned as the Hollywood press began to ask some awkward questions. Much of the wide-eyed enthusiasm that cast and crew had had going into this project had eroded into anger and resentment. But for every person who relates a story of abuse or being dangerously overworked, someone else is willing to say, sure it was tough but it was worth it and I never felt abused in the least.

During the shooting of the death and resurrection scene of Lindsay, Mary Elizabeth Mastrantonio finally snapped when the camera ran out of film in the middle of her most heart-wrenchingly dramatic moment. Cameron insisted on doing it again, even though several usable takes had already been captured. Mastrantonio, who was asked to sit around and wait while the film magazine was changed, stormed off the set, screaming, "We're not animals!"

The Abyss firmly established the notion that James Cameron was a holy terror, a megalomaniac with tunnel vision. From *The Abyss* on, this reputation would double with each movie he made.

Beleaguered *Abyss* crew members began to come up with the "James Cameron joke of the day." One of the jokes had Cameron dressing down a crew member who had the audacity to ask if he could go to the bathroom. Cameron screams at the unfortunate worker: "I'm letting you breathe! What more do you want?"

This treatment even extended to Cameron's brother, Mike, who was asked to appear in one scene. Mike Cameron still harbors mixed emotions about this incident. "I'll never forget this because it is the most putrid memory I have. Jim asks me if I want to be in one of the creepier scenes in the movie. I say, 'Sure, man' — then he tells me that he wants me to play a corpse in the downed atomic submarine. He tells me that the scene will be shot in twenty-five feet of water and that I'll have my eyes wide open throughout the entire shot because I'm dead. He then tells me that I will have to hold a live crab in my mouth so that when 'action' is called I open my mouth and the crab swims out. I did five takes and during two of them I bit down on the crab and crushed it because it was taking too long to set up the shot. It was really a nightmare. I enjoyed every minute of it."

When principal photography on *The Abyss* finally ended, the real struggle began. The pressure being exerted by the studio was increasing. Cameron and his crew were being asked to get the movie into theaters quickly to grab some of that lucrative summer box-office market share. The main problem facing Cameron now was that he had shot a few endings, each more radical than the next. One had the aliens saving Bud and then the disabled *Deepcore* as well. This is the ending that made it into the theaters. The more elaborate ending involved the aliens threatening mankind by creating looming tidal waves all over the world only to make them recede once it becomes apparent that humanity has got their message. This more philosophical ending was the one that Cameron favored: "It was a strange spot to be in. I had shot some very large, very expensive scenes for an ending that I wanted for the movie. But by having that ending I would be delivering a movie that would

be considerably longer than the running time I had contractually agreed to. The studio wanted the movie to be two
hours and no more. I thought I would test my version and
hope that the audience would flip for it, thus swaying the
studio's thinking, but ..."

Dallas, Texas was selected for the first sneak preview
showing of *The Abyss*. It was shown to a "cold" audience —
they knew they were coming for a first look at a major
motion picture but weren't told what it was. The version of
the movie they were shown contained a long subplot concerning political machinations that would put the world at
the brink of a nuclear exchange. The seabound aliens rescue Bud after he disarms the warhead that was threatening
them. This is the version that was ultimately saved for the
special director's cut on laser disc and the special videocassette version that was released in late 1996. This version is
certainly the more interesting one; it gives the movie a
classic science fiction feel, reminiscent of Robert Wise's
ingenious 1951 classic, *The Day the Earth Stood Still*. When
Cameron describes his movie, the depth of his feeling for
the story he is telling surfaces. "The story that I wanted to
tell, the ultimate goal of the film, was to tell the story of a
kind of apocalypse in which we are all judged by a supe-
rior race and found to be worthy of salvation because of a
single man, an average man, an Everyman, who represents
the good in all of us. The capacity to love is measured by
our willingness to sacrifice ourselves.

"The final sequence was really the heart of the whole film. That divine image of the huge waves suspended above the shore is an image straight out of my dreams. It is the source of inspiration for the entire film. It's been a nightmare of mine throughout my entire life, a vast wave rolling towards the shore, miles high, turning day into night. That dream, in my subconscious, became inextricably interwoven with the dread of death, and the specific dread of nuclear holocaust."

That final sequence with the tidal waves was the very one that divided the Dallas preview audience. Half loved the sequence and the other half were completely bewildered by it. Many stated that they felt the sequence was out of place, that it appeared to be taking place in an entirely different movie. Their reactions placed Cameron in the unpleasant position of having to consider compromising his vision.

Since Cameron had a final-cut contract, Fox could tell him to shorten the running time of the movie but they could not tell him what he had to remove. The studio had already backed Cameron to the tune of $50 million and had been very supportive throughout the project, so Cameron felt that he had to play ball. What he was to do would stun everyone involved in the project. Cameron decided to completely excise the tidal wave sequences that he had fought so hard to shoot.

This was both a bizarre decision and the absolutely

correct one. The talents of many people and a great deal of money had gone into making this sequence. Industrial Light & Magic were responsible for most of the visuals, while the famed surfing photographer Yuri Farrant had gone to Waimea, Hawaii, to shoot footage of huge waves rolling in. The elements were turned over to motion-control expert Paul Haliton, who rejigged them to produce the final sequence that was cut into the film.

Fox executives were dumbfounded by Cameron's decision and reluctant to lose the stunning visual effects. Fox countered by suggesting to Cameron that he remove the love-rekindling sequences involving Bud and Lindsay. Cameron stuck to his original plan, although he now admits, "At that point I think I was starting to lose my objectivity. It made perfect sense to remove the drowning sequence with Bud and Lindsay, as that was the only part that was completely divergent from the storyline. I had never used a test screening process before to base my decision on, but this time I was becoming completely reliant on the process."

Cameron had gone ahead and cut the movie down to two hours and twenty minutes from two hours and forty-seven minutes. The studio had their hearts set on a two-hour release, because anything longer threatens to lessen the number of showings in a day. Fox agreed to test the movie again. If the audience responded well to this new cut, they were prepared to release *The Abyss* at this somewhat extended running time.

This second audience, this time in California, were advised that they would see "the new James Cameron movie" — the house was in effect papered with Cameron fans. Not surprisingly, their reactions were overwhelmingly positive.

Competition was stiff in the summer of 1989. In June, Tim Burton's sensationally dark version of *Batman* was released to rave reviews and record box-office returns after an ingenious ad campaign that was to set standards for aggressiveness in marketing movies. *Batman* shattered all domestic box-office records and raised financial expectations for big-budget summertime movie releases. June also saw the release of *Star Trek V: The Final Frontier*, a franchise that can always be counted on to attract summer or Christmas-season teenaged movie dollars like a magnet. In July, *Lethal Weapon 2*, the sequel to the hit 1987 cop movie, was released and became even a bigger hit than its predecessor.

By the time *The Abyss* hit the theaters on August 9 it needed to work twice as hard and be twice as good to attract the kind of audiences that Cameron wanted and Twentieth Century Fox needed. The critical response to the movie was generally mixed. *Variety* said, "A first-rate underwater suspenser with an otherworldly twist, *The Abyss* suffers from a payoff unworthy of its buildup ... James Cameron delivers riveting, supercharged action segments only to get soggy when the aliens turn out to be friendly ... Almost all the action is exceedingly well rendered by Cameron and crew, with layers of tension woven into the plot until the experience becomes engulfing and nearly exhausting. Yet when the pic arrives at its major metaphorical question — what lies at the bottom of the abyss — it founders. Cameron hasn't got the answers, only a vague, optimistic suggestion." The *New York Times* echoed these sentiments, only with a bit more vitriol: "The best way to enjoy this overwrought action film is to go in knowing it is spectacularly silly — something the writer and director James Cameron never concedes. Fortunately, Mr. Cameron offsets his pretentious themes with luminous underwater photography, extraordinary special effects and countless near-catastrophes ... While *Aliens* had a campy edge to its stock lines, no one puts much spin on the wretched dialogue of *The Abyss*, they are too busy marveling at the ET's." The movie opened with a $9.3-million weekend gross and finished its domestic run with a disappointing $54-million take.

It was not until after the huge success of *Terminator 2: Judgment Day* two years later that Cameron assembled a director's cut, *The Abyss: The Special Edition*. He had just signed a production/development deal for his company Lightstorm Entertainment with Twentieth Century Fox worth an astounding $500 million. The arrangement also gave him the weight to put a movie into play without studio approval. The first project he decided on was *The Abyss: The Special Edition*. This plan was not the self-indulgent whim that it appeared to some. James Cameron recalls his thinking at the time: "It was really a no-win situation. If we release a special edition and it flops then we've bombed twice with the same movie. If we release it and it turns out to be a huge success then we look like dopes for not putting out this version in the first place. I had to look at this project objectively for the first time. It wasn't just a matter of throwing every foot of film we shot back into it. I knew that it had to be a good movie or there would be no point at all in doing it."

The Abyss: The Special Edition proved to bring its own set of problems to the table. Reassembled footage didn't match scenes from the completed print, so actors had to be brought back in to re-record their dialogue so it all flowed smoothly. Original music scorer Alan Silvestri was asked to do some more music for the additional scenes, but he was contracted out to another movie and couldn't accept Cameron's offer, so Robert Garrett, a longtime musician friend of Cameron's, was brought in. This task also proved daunting, since Cameron had added footage to some scenes to make them longer, meaning that the music now had gaps in it that Garrett had to bridge seamlessly. All the wrinkles were eventually worked out, with Cameron supervising every aspect of the new cut.

The Abyss: The Special Edition was released in pristine form on laser disc to across-the-board positive critical reaction. The laser disc market is growing but remains somewhat limited to hardcore film fans. The initial appeal was laser's ability to release movies in their correct aspect ratio, meaning they appear on the TV screen exactly as they appeared on the big screen, but VHS has since responded with its own "widescreen" or "letterboxed" versions of movies. Because so much information can be packed onto laser discs, filmmakers can release alternative versions of their movies along with documentary footage on the making of the movie all in the same package. This supplementary material on the laser disc *The Abyss: The Special Edition* is compelling to watch.

It has to be said that the longer version of *The Abyss* is the more satisfying of the two. The shortcomings of both were mitigated by the sheer virtuosity of Cameron's visual ideas and the stunning effects that created them. Without the final tidal wave scenes, the film resembled several other isolationist horror/science fiction movies that came before it, like *The Thing* (both the 1951 version and John Carpenter's 1982 remake) and Ridley Scott's *Alien.*

Cameron's storyline and characters may not be terribly original but his ability to create tension and suspense is without peer. The sequence in which the huge crane is ripped free in the storm and plunges into the water right over where *Deepcore* is anchored is a triumph of visual tension. And the water-based aliens are a uniquely fascinating creation. Criticize if you will, but it must be conceded that James Cameron pours his heart and soul into every scene of every movie he makes. This is not a statement that can be applied to many Hollywood filmmakers.

The Abyss will go down in cinematic history as one of the toughest shoots ever. Was it worth it? Cameron responds, "What it comes down to is that I simply couldn't *not* do it. I had to see this movie and the only way to see it was to go out and make it. Would I go through that whole experience again knowing what I know now? Absolutely."

Eight

TERMINATOR REDUX: THE MAKING OF *TERMINATOR 2: JUDGMENT DAY*

"Hasta la vista, baby."
ARNOLD SCHWARZENEGGER, *TERMINATOR 2: JUDGMENT DAY*

Los Angeles, 2029. Charred ruins fill the screen. Sarah Connor's voice tells us that on August 29, 1997, an atomic war erupted and killed more than 3 billion people. John Connor is the leader of the human resistance forces fighting the ground war against the ruling high-tech fighting machines that started the war. Sarah tells us that in 1984 a

Terminator was sent back in time to kill her to prevent her unborn son from becoming the great military leader that he is. A soldier was also sent back in time to protect her from this Terminator. The Terminator failed his mission. Now two more Terminators are being sent back in time, one with a mission to kill the young John Connor and the other to protect him and ensure he grows into manhood. Which will get to him first?

An electrical disturbance between two parked transport trucks leaves the naked Terminator (Arnold Schwarzenegger) in its wake. He strolls off in search of clothing and weapons as a second electrical disturbance in another part of Los Angeles leaves behind a second Terminator, a newer model T-1000 (Robert Patrick). A police officer happens along and the electrical disturbance catches his eye. As he investigates, the T-1000 quickly dispatches him and relieves him of his uniform and his squad car.

We are next introduced to the teenaged John Connor (Edward Furlong), a grungy, insolent kid living in foster care. His mother, Sarah Connor (Linda Hamilton), is being held at the Pescadero Psychiatric Institution by order of the court. She is now a tightly muscled ball of aggression who is psychologically and physically abused by the staff.

The two Terminators arrive at a mall where they have tracked John Connor. The T-1000 closes in on him first, but the Terminator arrives just in time to illustrate to us that he is the young man's protector. A vicious hand-to-hand fight ensues after they have exhausted all the ammo in their extensive arsenals. John escapes the scrum but is picked up by the Terminator on his Harley. The T-1000 gives chase in a transport-sized tow truck. This chase ends when the tow truck slams into the side of a bridge and explodes. The T-1000 strides out of the flames in a gleaming liquid-metal form. The Terminator explains the situation to John, who has heard from his mother the strange story of what happened in 1984. At John's suggestion they head to Pescadero to break Sarah out.

The T-1000 is also on his way to Pescadero, and he gets there first. The sequences of the shape-shifting liquid-metal T-1000 making his way through the state mental hospital in various incarnations are visually dazzling, and unlike anything ever before shown on the screen. At one point in the sequence the T-1000 becomes part of the checkered floor and in another sequence he is absorbed by iron bars so that he can pass through them.

When John and the Terminator arrive, Sarah is thrown into a state of terrified confusion. The Terminator extends a hand to her and says, "Come with me if you want to live," exactly what her protector, Reese, said to her in the first movie. Sarah, John, and the Terminator head into the desert to seek sanctuary and regroup. She questions the Terminator about the unfolding of history, and the Terminator explains that Miles Dyson (Joe Morton) of Cyberdyne Systems is unwittingly responsible for developing the supercomputer that nearly destroys the world. Dyson is a genius who develops the next wave of technology without considering the consequences.

In the desert Sarah, John, and the Terminator meet up with a shady group of Central American rebels led by a Spanish-speaking mercenary named Enrique (Castulo Guerra) who helps them arm themselves to the teeth. Sarah falls asleep and finds herself in the midst of a dream that has her in a children's playground on a sunny day. Suddenly an atomic bomb hits and Los Angeles is destroyed in several scenes of breathtaking devastation. Sarah awakens with a start and with a singular purpose. She heads off in the car alone. John and the Terminator quickly deduce that she is going to kill Miles Dyson before he invents his computer and thus change the future.

At Dyson's house Sarah sets up a vantage point and tries to shoot him from a distance. She wounds him in the shoulder but then quickly realizes that she is far too humane to finish him off. John and the Terminator arrive and try to explain this fantastic story to the incredulous Dyson. The Terminator gives Dyson a demonstration in the form of peeling the artificial flesh from his arm to expose the steel endoskeleton, like the one encased in the vault at Cyberdyne Systems that we have seen in an earlier scene. Dyson is convinced and agrees to help them destroy all the files and computer disks and the pieces of the first Terminator that he has been basing his research on.

At Cyberdyne a silent alarm has been tripped and a massive show of police power moves in and surrounds the building. A huge firefight takes place in which hundreds of rounds of ammo and numerous grenades are expended. Miles Dyson is killed seconds after he detonates a home-made bomb that wipes out all remaining traces of the research on the supercomputer, and half the building along with it.

The T-1000 arrives on the scene but Sarah, John and the Terminator have already escaped in a van. In a stunning piece of stunt work, the T-1000 rides his stolen police motorcycle to an upper floor of the building and jumps it to a hovering helicopter.

After a deliriously exciting van/helicopter chase they end up in a steel mill where the Terminator jumps onto a liquid nitrogen tanker and steers it inside a cavernous working steel plant. He sees to it that the tanker flips over and splits in two, causing the liquid nitrogen to spill out. The liquid-metal T-1000 is frozen solid as the nitrogen washes over him, and the Terminator blasts him with a shotgun, shattering him like a porcelain doll.

This is another of Cameron's false endings. The heat from the molten steel thaws the liquid metal enough for the T-1000 to reconstitute. He then chases the trio into a final battle that pushes the reaches of cinematic technology to new limits. The T-1000 meets his end after being blown into a vat of bubbling molten steel and being completely absorbed by it.

To rid the present of any threat from the future, the Terminator instructs Sarah to lower him into the vat of molten steel as well. He cannot do it himself because his program doesn't allow him to self-destruct. The Terminator's final scenes with John are remarkably poignant, given the nature of the movie. The Terminator slowly sinks into the molten metal, giving the thumbs-up sign just before he disappears completely.

Terminator 2: Judgment Day is an action movie of remarkable depth, humor, and, surprisingly enough, humanity, but it is the advancement of cinematic visual effects that audiences remember long after they leave the theater.

Screenwriter William Wisher first met James Cameron through mutual friend Randal Frakes when they were both eighteen years old in Orange County, California. Wisher was an aspiring actor and Cameron was an aspiring artist. The two hit it off almost immediately and have remained friends ever since.

When Cameron was getting his thoughts together on the original *Terminator* he called Wisher, and the two of them bounced some ideas off one another. Cameron liked what he heard and asked Wisher if he wanted to contribute a couple of scenes to the screenplay. Wisher wrote some of the earlier scenes of Sarah being questioned at the police station. In addition to this Cameron asked Wisher and Frakes to pen the mass-market novelization of the *Terminator* screenplay.

After *The Terminator* took the world by storm, Wisher and Cameron started talking about a sequel. Several ideas were tossed around and some plans were made, but nothing took hold. Then one night Cameron asked Wisher to drop by his house to talk about a *Terminator* sequel yet again. Wisher went but he wasn't optimistic that anything would come of the meeting. Years later Wisher still remembers the inauspicious birth of one of the biggest movies in history. "Jim pulled this old yellow sheet of paper out of a notebook; he handed it to me without saying anything. There was one sentence scribbled on the dog-eared page that was written quite a while ago. It read: 'Young John Connor and the Terminator that comes back to befriend him.'"

Wisher reacted to the idea with a laugh, until Cameron told him that a *Terminator* sequel was indeed coming together and that this was the idea he had decided to base it on.

The two holed up in Cameron's house to write the screenplay, hunched in front of a computer screen, taking turns sketching out scenes and elements that they would each like to see go into the scenes. Wisher recalls, "Every time we would get an idea we'd open a computer file and store the idea under the title of the scene. As more ideas came to us, we would separate them into these little files.

When we had enough of these files we put them all together in a treatment."

The pair then separated the task into two parts; William Wisher took the first part of the story and James Cameron took the second half. Since the treatment was already well fleshed out, it was simply a matter of reformatting and filling in the blanks.

As is the case with most sequels to hit movies, the challenge was to make sure they didn't repeat themselves. Cameron and Wisher moved their thinking in a different direction — more toward a direct linear continuation to the story rather than go the traditional sequel route of rehashing the original story or writing a completely unrelated story that cashes in on an identifiable title (*Speed* and *Speed 2*, for example).

The pair decided that *T2* would take place about twelve years after audiences saw Linda Hamilton drive off toward Mexico at the end of the first movie. Cameron and Wisher had to think about what Sarah had gone through in the intervening years. She would still be heavily saddled with memories of the horribly traumatic events she had experienced in *The Terminator*, but she would also have matured. In the words of William Wisher, "The original *Terminator*, to me, was the perfect movie. This is going to sound funny, but to me *The Terminator* is very much like *It's a Wonderful Life* — it's a story that says your life, every life, could make a difference. On the surface you're a nobody, but on some other level you could be the most important person on earth. People can't help but love that kind of story."

Four weeks after first sitting down to write, Cameron and Wisher had completed a forty-page treatment. They had everything laid out except the dialogue. Once the dialogue was added the pair realized that they had written a movie that would cost at least $200 million to make. Wisher says, "We really had to tighten it up. We had to look at what would be the most expensive aspects of the movie, which was the T-1000. We went over the script and asked ourselves if it was necessary to show the shape change as many times as we did."

Length was also a problem. As written, the movie would be about three and a half hours long, and had to be shortened by at least a couple of major sequences. One of these took place at a desert camp where Sarah had gone for survival training. Returning to the camp after breaking out of Pescadero, she seeks the help of an ex-Marine mercenary who had been her teacher. Though this scene contributed to Sarah's character development, it and the character of the mercenary were deleted from the script.

Another excised scene involved an emotional meeting between the adult John Connor and his father, Kyle Reese. This was the goodbye scene that Reese talked about in the first movie, when John sent him back in time. Reese, of course, doesn't know that he is John's father, while John knows that he is sending Reese to his death and is trying not to let his emotions show. Notwithstanding the scene's poignancy, Wisher admits, "That scene is the kind of thing that a writer will miss but an audience never will."

When the decision was made to recast Arnold Schwarzenegger as the Terminator, who is now a benevolent force, a problem arose: how do you come up with a villain intimidating enough to make a convincing adversary to Schwarzenegger? They toyed with the idea of having Schwarzenegger play both Terminators, but that was quickly discarded because neither writer could figure out how to make Arnold able to intimidate Arnold. They then considered a super-Terminator, a physically larger Terminator with much of the same powers as its predecessors. They settled on an idea that Cameron had had for the original movie. Before Schwarzenegger was cast in the first *Terminator*, Cameron had envisioned the cyborg as an "infiltrator unit" of average human size and proportions. They decided to make the T-1000 smaller, faster, and a lot more advanced than his adversary.

Cameron and his casting people looked at hundreds of professional child actors before casting the completely inexperienced and virtually unknown fourteen-year-old Edward Furlong of Pasadena in the role of the young John Connor. Casting director Mali Finn showed Cameron a tape of Furlong because, even though he was inexperienced, he showed a quality of genuineness that was unusual. Finn had not been able to describe the "it" she saw, but Cameron looked at the tape and saw "it" immediately. He agreed that there was something right about Furlong. Even though Furlong didn't have a clue how to act and fumbled through his audition, Cameron continued to come back to the boy when he was thinking about casting the role. In spite of his awkwardness and inexperience, Furlong cried convincingly, and Cameron was persuaded that he could be coached to carry off the poignant scenes in the script. Cameron knew he was taking a chance: "Every actor I saw after Eddie seemed fake by comparison. Even the ones that I had liked before seemed fake to me. So I kept coming back to him four or five times. I finally simply said, let's do it."

Edward Furlong had not a shred of acting experience, nor any desire to act, when Mali Finn picked him out of a local boys' club. Furlong describes the day Mali Finn discovered him: "She was looking for someone who looked a bit like Michael Biehn and Linda Hamilton and she just found me at the boys' club. The funny thing about it was that I didn't even want to go to the boys' club that day, but my uncle, who I lived with, made me go. I was talking to some friends and Mali came up to me and asked me if I wanted to try out for this part. She took a Polaroid of me and I went home and told my aunt and uncle. They thought it was some weird X-rated thing, but Mali called them and told them that it was *T2* and my aunt, right away, knew it was going to be a really big movie."

Furlong did a taped audition with Finn, and Cameron was impressed enough to set up a second audition, this time with Linda Hamilton. Furlong knew he was on shaky ground: "That audition didn't go so well because I was nervous about working with Linda. After that audition I thought there was no way I was going to get the role."

Cameron assigned a dialogue coach to Furlong, and after the young actor had worked with her for a while Cameron auditioned him again. This time he performed much better. Cameron informed the young man that he would call him in a few days with his decision. To Furlong's shock Cameron called him later that same day to tell him he had the part.

Furlong's first day on the set was a classic introduction to the world of moviemaking James Cameron–style. After Furlong did his first scene, Cameron watched the playback. Something looked wrong. Furlong had put on lip balm and it made his lips look unnaturally shiny on film. Cameron tore a strip off Furlong because they had to shoot the sequence again from scratch. Furlong was able to repeat the scene to Cameron's satisfaction, but the experience left an indelible impression on the novice actor. And it was certainly not the last time that Cameron would lose his cool with his young co-star.

Cameron has described this leap of faith in Furlong as the single scariest creative decision of the entire film. All the time and all the money would go right out the window if young Furlong didn't work out.

When developing the role of John Connor, Wisher and Cameron ran into a troubling problem. The boy was written as being not only familiar with firearms but skilled in using them, an idea that audiences might find objectionable. "We really had to feel our way through that one," says Wisher. "What we finally came up with was John's indifference to guns. He knows about guns but he is indifferent to them. There are no scenes with John blowing people away or anything like that, although we thought at one point we might have a scene where he threatens people with weapons. But we ultimately realized that that would just be too much. We wrote in one scene where Sarah tries to give him a gun and he refuses to take it."

From the outset, Cameron was firm in his conviction that he would cancel the entire project altogether if either Arnold Schwarzenegger or Linda Hamilton weren't available or willing to do it. Schwarzenegger had talked to Cameron about a sequel well before the first *Terminator* even came out. Hamilton had also discussed the project with Cameron over the years. But Cameron need not have worried about either of these scenarios playing out. Both Schwarzenegger and Hamilton were so pumped up by the idea of reprising their roles that they both agreed to do the movie without seeing a script or a treatment.

Cameron had told *T2* co-producer Mario Kassar that he would not write one word of the screenplay and would not commit to the idea of making the sequel until Linda

Hamilton was signed on because to Cameron her character was as essential as Schwarzenegger's. At this point
Cameron had not spoken to Hamilton in a couple of
years. He tracked her down, reaching her on the very day
she was about to take a leading role in another high-profile science fiction movie, and pitched the idea to her out
of the blue. The problem was that Cameron had nothing
to offer her in the way of a script other than "Your son is
the target and you are in a mental hospital. The kid teams
up with a good Terminator, they break you out of the
mental hospital, then you all save the world." Based on
this slim outline, Hamilton immediately turned down the
other role.

A month would go by before a deal could be worked
out with Hamilton. That was fine with Cameron; that was
another month he could avoid writing.

Linda Hamilton, who would become romantically
involved with Cameron during the making of *T2*, was eager
to step into what she would later describe as the "toughest
physical role I can imagine." She had always been confident that a second *Terminator* movie would be made.
"My instinct told me that there would be a *Terminator 2*
some day, even though it did take a long time. Jim credited the success of *Aliens*, given the fact that it was also a
sequel made years after the original, for his being allowed
to make another *Terminator*. So I know he didn't consider
the timeline much of an obstacle. There was really no time

restriction on making the movie, so when it finally came together I wasn't surprised at all."

Hamilton was a young, less-experienced actor when she played Sarah Connor in the first film, which suited the requirements of that role. In the time between the movies, Hamilton had matured as an actor and as a person. When it came time to reprise Sarah Connor, she, like her character, was tougher, wiser, and more determined. "Like Sarah, at the time of *T2* I had a son that I was raising alone. So I found the character easy to grasp."

James Cameron wanted to make some major changes to the character of Sarah, and Linda Hamilton was in complete agreement. He introduced the notion early on that he might write her as being insane. Hamilton liked the idea but was concerned about playing a character who was feral and nasty.

T2 revealed a Sarah Connor who had gone through a complete physical transformation. She had become schooled in the use of weapons and combat techniques, and boasted a lean, strong, well-muscled physique. Hamilton prepared by spending four months undergoing her own rigorous physical training regimen. "As soon as I read the script I realized that I would have to commit myself to really getting into shape. I began working out with a physical trainer six mornings a week, two to three hours a day. I lifted weights and did aerobics. It was really wonderful to see myself transformed, and I was a hundred times stronger

than I had ever been. That was a good thing because I
never would have made it through the film otherwise. I was
battered and chased and slammed into walls and everything
else. Every day was a physical challenge, but I was prepared for it. I was as much of an Arnold Schwarzenegger
as I could be."

Hamilton also underwent military-style instruction
with a commando trainer to learn how to handle herself in
hand-to-hand combat. She describes the mixed feelings
she had during this period. "I did that for two months and
they were the longest two months of my life. I was ready
to quit at any time but I didn't, because I knew this was a
process that had to be gone through. So even though the
training was very hard, it helped me focus on Sarah and
really understand her. She doesn't have time in her life for
an expression or a smile. She's all business."

A tiny shred of a love story provided Hamilton with a
much-needed break from the physical demands of her role.
It was a dream sequence that involved Reese coming back
to pay her one last visit. Everyone agreed that it had to be
a powerful and passionate scene, for Sarah's love for Reese
is what has kept her going. The scene was shot in the middle of the schedule after a lot of major action sequences
had already been filmed. Linda Hamilton had been beaten
up and thrown around and was exhausted by the time this
scene was shot. "I couldn't stop crying," she recalls.

This scene was the only one that Michael Biehn was

asked to appear in. He was first approached about making this appearance during the shooting of *The Abyss*, but at that time he wasn't all that optimistic about being in the second *Terminator* movie. "Jim and I both thought about it and tossed several ideas around, but we couldn't come up with a way to bring the character back. So I knew early on that I wouldn't be involved with the sequel."

But as the *T2* screenplay developed, Cameron started thinking that a dream sequence or flashback would be an excellent way to inject some romance into the film. When this idea was put to Michael Biehn, he immediately accepted a role that was little more than a cameo. Biehn has always maintained that the romantic aspect was his favorite part of playing Reese. He also holds Cameron in high regard. "I owe much of my career to Jim Cameron," says Biehn. "If he asked me to mow his lawn for him, I'd do it." Ironically, this was one of the first sequences Cameron left on the cutting room floor, although it was later restored for the expanded versions on laser disc and videocassette.

All the actors in *Terminator 2: Judgment Day* felt the film was something of a homecoming. Linda Hamilton has stated that she came to respect James Cameron a lot more during the making of *T2*. She hadn't fully realized what a talented visionary he was during their first experience together. Hamilton, who later became Cameron's live-in lover and mother to his daughter, made a remark during the making of *T2* that was a precursor to their relationship.

"Working with Jim on *Terminator 2*, I felt very well partnered. He made me feel nurtured and appreciated and, unlike the experience on the first film, made me feel that I was working with him as a real collaborator."

For Arnold Schwarzenegger, there was never much doubt that the Terminator would be resurrected in one form or another. The two men had made an agreement that no matter what happened it could not be made unless both were involved. Schwarzenegger recalls that *T2* came together with difficulty: "We realized that there were a lot of negative influences involved at this point. We wanted to make sure that no one would split us up or do their own little things."

Hemdale Film Corporation was one of those negative influences. Hemdale had backed the first film because it fell in line with their philosophy of making movies fast and cheap. This attitude doesn't imply a lack of commitment to quality or vision; they simply didn't have access to major-studio-sized finances. They were insisting that any *Terminator* sequel be made on this same scale, even though early plans for *T2* were much more ambitious, not to mention more expensive, than the original movie. Since Hemdale was, in part, in control of the sequel rights, it looked uncertain early on that a second movie would ever be made. Gale Anne Hurd also partly controlled the sequel rights, and she was both too busy and disinclined to work with Cameron again. Had she not agreed to deal her rights to the sequel away to the eventual producers, for a rumored $5 million, then no one would be making a second *Terminator*.

Neither Cameron nor Arnold Schwarzenegger would make a deal with Hemdale. As the years went by, Schwarzenegger grew into one of the biggest box-office draws in the world, with several worldwide hits (*Commando, Predator, Twins,* and *Total Recall,* to name a few). And James Cameron became a highly bankable director. The allure of these two mega-talents became too attractive to resist. The high-profile, free-spending Carolco Pictures, headed by Mario Kassar and Andrew Vajna, stepped up and bought out the Hemdale interest. The most expensive movie to date, *Terminator 2: Judgment Day,* was in motion.

Cameron had actually committed himself to having the script finished by the time the Carolco team boarded a private jet for the 1990 Cannes Film Festival, where *Terminator 2* was to be announced to the world. Cameron ended up cutting this right down to the wire. The airport limousine was idling in his driveway when Cameron hit the print command on the computer. He had been writing for thirty-six straight hours. The second the final page rolled out of the printer, he stuffed the script into his briefcase and headed for the airport. Cameron was so dog-tired that he collapsed into sleep as soon as the plane was in the air. Arnold Schwarzenegger was reading the script for the first time, and as the plane bounced and rocked its way through the night sky he was riveted by what he was reading. Once they were on the ground Schwarzenegger told Cameron that the script was all that he had hoped for and more.

At Cannes the announcement was made that *Terminator 2: Judgment Day* would be in theaters by July 4, 1991. Cameron had just over thirteen months to deliver the most technologically advanced movie in history and all he had in hand was a first-draft screenplay.

He flew back to Los Angeles and immediately started work, both on mounting the mammoth movie and on rewriting the screenplay. His final version of the screenplay would be the version that was shot almost without alteration. A scene was trimmed here and there, dialogue was nipped and tucked, but he basically shot the screenplay as is. The last bit of writing on *T2*, the voice-over narration at the end of the film, was done less than one month before the release of the movie.

Schwarzenegger had always entertained the notion of playing both Terminators. The year before the *T2* deal was made, both he and Cameron were at the Cannes Film Festival, and Cameron told the actor that he had completely rethought the premise they had originally discussed. Cameron told him flat out that he didn't want him to play both Terminators because that would limit the story. Schwarzenegger understood Cameron's concern and willingly went along with what the director proposed. He explains, "Jim is someone I respect very much. When you trust someone, you trust their talent. It's not necessary to question things that much. If Jim was comfortable with the decision then so was I."

Schwarzenegger's respect for Cameron would grow while the movie was being shot. "Working with Jim Cameron is unique because he is basically everything!" says the actor. "He writes the screenplay, he comes up with the concept, he directs the scenes. He wants to do his own lighting and he wants to work the camera himself. He wants to do everything. You see him using the smoke machine and you see him putting on the blood and trying to do your makeup even though the makeup and special effects people have done it already. But he has to try and improve on it somehow. So he really has his fingers in every aspect of the movie. That is why a Jim Cameron movie has that look, that special, unique look."

The decision to make the evil T-1000 a slightly built shape-shifting liquid-metal malevolence meant the role would have to be cast with particular care. In the end it went to a fellow Corman alumnus, Robert Patrick.

Robert Patrick left his home in Cleveland in 1988 to try to make it as an actor in Hollywood, but he succeeded only in playing bad-guy roles in Roger Corman's low-budget films. To secure the T-1000 role, Patrick met with Mali Finn to do a video screen test that James Cameron would review. As usual, Cameron had decided to shroud the project in absolute secrecy, so Patrick was given only vague instructions during the test and was not told the exact nature of the character. "All my agent told me was to be the most intense, scariest, fearsome guy I could be," says Patrick.

James Cameron was impressed with Patrick's audition tape, so he called him back the next day for another test, this time under his own direction. The two hit it off right away with their shared experience of going through the Roger Corman College of Moviemaking. But it still wasn't a done deal. Cameron showed Patrick some storyboards and told him a few specifics about the role. The secrecy notwithstanding, Patrick was infected with Cameron's enthusiasm. There was still another audition and several more meetings before the role was finally handed to Patrick, who immediately went out and hired a personal trainer. He was determined to get himself into the best shape he had ever been in. "I did that physical stuff on my own," he recalls, "as character development. I learned to control my body. How to stretch it out and make it look fluid. I even changed my breathing. My trainer suggested I go through workouts breathing only through my nose. I found that breathing through my nose even while running very fast helped to create this machine-like quality in the T-1000."

Patrick also trained with Linda Hamilton's trainer, Uzi Gal. By the time the cameras rolled, the actor was in peak mental and physical condition. Because there wasn't a lot of dialogue to his role, he knew he would have to rely on physical presence to impart his character.

One of the most difficult aspects of *T2* for Patrick lay not in the script or in the training but in participating in fight scenes with Arnold Schwarzenegger. Patrick was scared to death of the physical confrontation. He had to go to great lengths to psych himself up for the first fight scene, convincing himself that he was a more advanced model than the Terminator and thus could hold his own with Arnold.

Like Patrick, young Eddie Furlong was also quite nervous when it came time to meet Arnold Schwarzenegger for the first time. "Once I got to know him better I wasn't nervous at all. He's not so special," says Furlong.

In fact, Schwarzenegger and Furlong got along so well that they often goofed around together on the set like a couple of teenaged buddies. Cameron would happen by and express his displeasure to Furlong. Arnold could turn it on and off. He could be Arnold one minute and the Terminator the next, but Furlong was too much of a neophyte to shift gears with the same ease. This shortcoming started to show up in the scenes they had together and Cameron wasn't amused. Furlong was officially instructed to avoid clowning around with Schwarzenegger during working hours.

Linda Hamilton became frustrated throughout the filming of *T2* because she had the feeling that it was turning into a big boys' club. She wasn't crazy about Schwarzenegger and remembers his "filthy sense of humor." She was forced to spend hours in a car in the desert with him and Furlong, and she describes the two as "about the same age emotionally. I would just sit there helplessly while Arnold was giving Eddie tips on women. It was excruciating."

Cameron had fallen for Hamilton during the making of the first *Terminator* and was living with her by the time the second film was made. Her strength was enormously appealing to him. Her willingness to be a thrill seeker drew him to her like a magnet. But even though they were living together, she still fell victim to his ruthless control over the film's final version. She resented his decision to cut the Reese/Sarah flashback that had wrung her out emotionally, as she believed the scene added depth and dimension. "I was told that these scenes were an interruption of the pace of the movie," she recalls. "The mood got tender and quiet and interrupted the buildup of the movie. Jim is an amazing editor; he can cut whole sections of the film that are absolutely brilliant, but if they hinder the pace of the movie then it is snip, snip, snip.

"I was sleeping with the man and he didn't tell me, until we were looping. There was so much that had gone into that love scene with Michael Biehn. You were brought into the open heart of the character, which is just never that wide open throughout the rest of the movie."

The day the Reese dream sequence was shot was surreal in several other respects. Just minutes before the shot was done word filtered onto the set that the United States was at war in the Persian Gulf and that targets in Kuwait and Iraq were being pounded by the first wave of a multinational assault force.

The mood on the set was somber. James Cameron set the scene, then quietly went behind the video monitor. He rolled the scene and called for action. Reese's last line was, "Remember the message: the future isn't set, there is no fate but what we make ourselves." *Cut.* Cameron headed over to his actors to fine-tune their performances. Those not directly involved gathered in small groups to share information about the state of the war. A Sony Watchman was pressed into service so the president's address to the nation could be watched.

The irony in another of Reese's lines was lost on no one: "There is not much time left in the world, Sarah," he says before being swallowed up by smoke.

Dreams play a key role in several of Cameron's movies, and it is not uncommon for him to incorporate his own dreams into his screenplays. Cameron describes the relationship to his dreams this way: "Dreams, in general, are very important to me. I think they are as significant as any other part of our daily reality, and certainly part of our psychological process. And, personally, dreams have played a crucial role in my creative process. When I was a kid I had a lot of dreams about nuclear war. I don't know what that says about me, but I'm sure that it has impacted on several of the movies that I've made."

Among the first creative team members to be signed on to *T2* was conceptual artist Steve Berg. Berg had been working on another project with James Cameron when *T2* fell into place. As usual Cameron had several designs and ideas in his head, and Berg's job was to refine them.

But when it came time to get the big effects under way Cameron went back to Stan Winston. Since their last collaboration, Winston had directed a few movies himself (*Pumpkinhead* and *The Adventures of a Gnome Named Gnorm*) and Cameron was afraid that Winston's days as strictly an effects man were over. Winston's reaction came as a welcome surprise. "When Jim Cameron came to me about doing *T2* my answer was an emphatic yes," says Winston. "I wouldn't want anyone else to do it because I feel a pride of ownership of the original Terminator. I also love working with Jim Cameron because he always makes our stuff look great. The best work we've done has been on James Cameron's movies."

The script was not even finished when Winston agreed to join the *T2* team. Winston and Cameron met at Cameron's house and the director described the story to him by enthusiastically acting out scenes. At this point in the development of the movie Winston's planned participation was crucial but not extensive. By the time the script was fully fleshed out, however, James Cameron and William Wisher had written what was accurately described as the biggest special effects movie ever attempted.

Winston recalls that "Jim came up with just hundreds of insane, impossible effects, which he always does. There were more effects written in the first two minutes of this movie than the entire first movie. But he had come up with such terrific ideas that we were really excited about the prospect of trying to do them."

Cameron called on Winston to direct a teaser trailer for the movie. Cameron didn't want it just to be some early footage from the movie; he wanted a separate bit of intrigue to draw the audience's attention to what he was doing without giving anything away. Winston took the $150,000 budget he was allotted and made something quite spectacular, a four-minute trailer that would let North American movie audiences know that the Terminator was coming back. Cameron was worried about audience reaction to Arnold Schwarzenegger returning in the same role when the cyborg had been clearly destroyed in the first film. What Winston and his team came up with was a trailer showing a futuristic assembly line churning out copy after copy of Terminators, all of which looked exactly like Schwarzenegger. It took five days to film the trailer and it dazzled audiences all over North America. It was brilliant in its simplicity, explaining quickly how Arnold could return, giving notice of another *Terminator*, and leaving the audience without a hint of what the new movie was about.

As was the case with *Aliens* and *The Abyss*, Cameron was faced with a very tight post-production time if *T2* was going to make it into the theaters in early summer, as planned. Cameron, as always, was calm and well organized. "The most important thing was to stay on top of it while we were shooting — editing scenes as they were being shot. I had to realize that I simply wasn't going to get a day off until the movie was in theaters — that was a given. It was not only a logistically difficult picture, a technologically difficult picture, and a dramatically difficult picture, but it also had to be done on a ridiculously short schedule. So, what else is new?"

Cameron's reputation as a tough taskmaster heightened on the set of *T2*. He offers no apologies for being exceptionally demanding of his crew and actors. "It's just part of the working process for me. Some people take it personally and some people don't. The ones who work with me again are the ones who don't. They realize that it is just a matter of trying to keep things moving and keep people on their toes and thinking.

"I'm always trying to think ahead — 'What hasn't been thought of? What hasn't been prepared? What could throw a monkey wrench into things three or four set-ups down the road?' I'm harsh on people because I want to inspire them to do their very best and think things through and not just coast and ask what time lunch is going to be. This is a business, not a party.

"Every time I start a film I have a fantasy that it will be like a big family and we'll have a good time and we'll all have these wonderfully creative moments together. But that isn't what filmmaking is. *It's war.* It's a group of human beings fighting against the tendency of the universe to become disorganized. Entropy is there every day, and you are struggling to make something out of it. For me, that's pretty much the filmmaking process in a nutshell."

When *Terminator 2: Judgment Day* was released to theaters on the July 4 weekend in 1991, it accounted for more than half of all the movie tickets sold in North America. But as wildly enthusiastically as this movie was received by audiences, it was not without its detractors, starting with the criticism that refashioning Schwarzenegger/the Terminator as a hero was a silly concept. Cameron counters by arguing that "the Terminators exist outside any moral framework, they're machines. It would be like saying one gun is a good gun and another gun is a bad gun."

T2 is certainly a festival of mayhem, like its predecessor, but the difference in this movie is that many more lighter touches have been added to the mix. It plays like a cross between a science fiction shocker and a picaresque comedy. Cameron builds the humor around the Terminator's being without any sense of human decorum, a deadpan automaton. A criticism that is often thrown at *T2* is that it made graphic cinematic violence commonplace. Terminator action figures were sold to kids who were not old enough to see the movie, and the film may have upped the ante for violent content in subsequent films.

Terminator 2: Judgment Day was the first movie to cost over $100 million to produce, then a landmark figure that has since been surpassed by several blockbusters. (In the summer of 1997 a staggering fifteen movies that cost over $100 million were scheduled for release.) Still, the *T2* endeavor wasn't as risky as the numbers suggest. The film was turning a profit before it hit the theaters through lucrative distribution deals.

In spite of the success of this sequel, Cameron doesn't like to repeat himself, and he decided to switch gears dramatically for his next movie. This time out, he would take his inspiration not from the dark reaches of his subconscious or his dreams but from a little-known French farce.

Nine

CAMERON TAKES MIAMI: THE MAKING OF *TRUE LIES*

"I let my wife strip for me ... I think those kinds of things keep a marriage alive."
ARNOLD SCHWARZENEGGER

After the astounding success of *Terminator 2: Judgment Day*, which pulled in over $200 million domestically alone, Cameron found himself at a crossroads. There was serious talk of a big-budget live-action version of *Spiderman*, but the project was deemed cost-prohibitive and beyond the reach of cinematic technology. MGM has recently purchased the rights to make *Spiderman*, and James Cameron's name has once again been mentioned in connection with it, but his schedule is set for at least the next four years. There was also talk of making *The Crowded Room*, a script Cameron wrote with actor/writer Todd Graff (Hippie in *The Abyss*) about the Billy Milligan multiple-personality defense case, but legal wranglings stalled that project so many times that Cameron eventually sold the rights to the script to Warner Bros., where director David Fincher (*Alien 3*) is said to be interested in it. Cameron also had trouble setting it up because it was outside the usual range of stories he had so successfully told up to this point. Then there was the staggering production deal Cameron and his Lightstorm Entertainment signed with Twentieth Century Fox worth a reported $500 million. The structure of the deal was testament to just how high on the Hollywood totem pole Cameron was now perched. Under the deal's terms, he was allowed to put any project he wanted into production without studio approval up to a budget of $70 million. He would have to seek out additional funding above that figure himself, but a side deal was struck with JVC in Japan to cover the overages.

After *Terminator 2*, Cameron's fourth science fiction movie in a row, he yearned to make something different; his radar was out for a challenge he hadn't attempted. That challenge was dropped in his lap by none other than Arnold Schwarzenegger.

True Lies is based on a 1991 French movie called *La*

Totale!, which is about a low-level bureaucrat who hides his clandestine life as a secret agent from his unsuspecting wife. It was actually Bobby Shriver, brother of Schwarzenegger's wife, Maria Shriver, who first told Schwarzenegger about *La Totale!* and was later rewarded with an "executive producer" credit for his efforts. Cameron and Schwarzenegger would often get together and go tearing around the canyons together on their motorcycles. They would stop at a joint called Patrick's Roadhouse to relax and talk a little business. It was during one of these outings that Schwarzenegger described the story of the French film to Cameron. Schwarzenegger and Cameron were both attracted to the storyline that involved a superhero who was off doing things that influenced world events but who could not handle, was indeed lost in, the smaller arena of his own marriage. (It is only speculation that part of the appeal of this story was that Arnold himself was married to a woman who spent more time with her family than with him.)

James Cameron was certainly up for it. "I had done big action pictures and I had done visual pictures, so from a cinematic standpoint there wasn't a lot of challenges left to explore. But comedy, that's a challenge of another sort, something entirely new for me."

This isn't to say that Cameron's other movies are entirely without humor. He had injected some laughs into *Aliens* and *The Abyss*, and the Terminator has his own deadpan charm, but this time he would have to write a funny script; he would need to have a confident grasp of a story based entirely on a humorous premise.

Cameron saw the potential in *La Totale!* but he knew that if he and Schwarzenegger were to team up again expectations would be very high indeed. He would have to turn a low-budget, small-scale French farce into a larger-than-life James Cameron blockbuster, with lots of high-intensity action set pieces.

He contacted his friend Randy Frakes about collaborating on the screenplay, and the two put together some ideas. Cameron was essentially using Frakes as a sounding board; when he had what he thought were enough ideas he went away and developed another of his novella-length treatments.

Visual effects ace John Bruno, who had won an Oscar for his work on *The Abyss*, was finishing up work on the Renny Harlin/Sylvester Stallone movie *Cliffhanger* at the Boss Film Studios when he received a call from James Cameron. Cameron wanted Bruno to help him come up with effects involving the high-tech Harrier jump jet used in the ending of *True Lies*.

Hero Harry Tasker (Schwarzenegger) uses the Harrier to destroy a nest of Crimson Jihad terrorists who have taken over a downtown Miami office tower. The Harrier rises to the top floors of the building in a vertical climb, then blasts out an entire floor, killing most of the horde of terrorists. In the meantime, Harry's daughter has been chased onto the roof by the head terrorist, Aziz (Art Malik), and is climbing out on a construction crane when Harry appears in the jet and shoots Aziz with a pistol. The terrorist falls to his death, Harry's daughter drops safely into his arms, and then Harry guides the Harrier to a safe landing on the street below. John Bruno read Cameron's technically complex ending expecting the worst, but he rose to the challenge: "I read it and I told Jim that I liked it, but I thought we should do more with the villain."

For the next few months Cameron and Bruno faxed script pages and sketches back and forth and had frequent phone conversations that lasted well into the night. It didn't take long for the ending sequence to be pushed right over the top by sheer enthusiasm alone. They finally decided to have Harry Tasker hover just beneath the construction crane and have his daughter drop down onto the nose of the jet. Then, as they start to pull away, the terrorist villain jumps onto the wing and works his way up to the cockpit, where he and Harry engage in a knife fight. The Harrier spins out of control and starts banging into the surrounding buildings, yet the combat inside the cockpit continues unabated. When Harry slams Aziz into the instrument panel it inadvertently launches a missile that destroys much of Miami.

After all this was written down Cameron stepped back and realized that his hero was doing more damage than the villain. They toned things down, which left them with the problem of what to do with the chief terrorist. John Bruno suggested that Aziz be hooked onto the missile and launched along with it into a helicopter carrying another set of his terrorists. Cameron rejigged this idea to have Aziz launched through the blown-out floor of the office tower into the helicopter that is on the other side of the building.

Cameron got a jump start in assembling his production team while the screenplay was still being formulated. He hired Stephanie Austin as producer, reprising her duties from *T2*. Peter Leonard, who was nominated for an Oscar for his work on *Aliens*, was brought back as production designer. Thomas Fisher and Joel Kramer were hired to oversee the nonstop physical effects and stunt work.

Mark Goldblatt, Conrad Buff, and Richard A. Harris, all Cameron veterans, were the editing team. Brad Fiedel, creator of the compelling music for both *Terminator* movies, was asked to come back and score the new movie. One new member of Team Cameron was Australian cinematographer Russell Carpenter, who was finishing up work on his first American movie, *Hard Target*, for Hong Kong–born action movie maestro John Woo.

True Lies would also be the first James Cameron movie tackled visually by Digital Domain, the effects company he co-founded. The founding of Digital Domain took Cameron another step up in the overall control he had in making his movies. "The tricky thing was trying to create this user-friendly effects facility from scratch and do a picture [*True*

Lies] at the same time," explains Cameron. "Industrial Light & Magic did it with *Star Wars*, but other people have tried it and it went nowhere."

Cameron and his new Digital Domain team had to find space to house the facilities, and they had to acquire the equipment, assemble talented personnel, concoct some sort of methodology, and test everything out. By the time that was all done and they were ready to start shooting, 90 percent of the available time was used up. But the pressure of having production schedules to meet did get Digital Domain off the ground a lot sooner than otherwise would have been possible.

John Bruno went straight from *Cliffhanger* to *True Lies*, working initially out of the new Lightstorm production offices in Santa Monica. Since the scenes involving the Harrier jets would be the most challenging, the storyboarding and painstakingly precise arranging of the elaborate shots began in earnest.

Bruno also faced the challenge of another sequence of visual virtuosity. Aziz and his mob have smuggled four nuclear weapons into the country and are transporting them along the causeway that connects the Florida Keys with the mainland. Harry Tasker calls in two Marine Corps Harrier jets to take the terrorists out. They achieve this by obliterating a section of the causeway with missiles.

Before work even began *True Lies* was being called Cameron's James Bond movie. But Cameron had a different approach to his movie. "The connection to James Bond is fairly obvious given that James Bond is such a clearly identifiable cultural icon. But to me *True Lies* is actually about the schizophrenic nature of marriage."

Cameron got even more personal about the *True Lies* storyline when asked what specifically appealed to him about the Bond reference. "When I was a kid I loved all the James Bond movies, I just loved all of them. I also ate up *The Man from U.N.C.L.E.* and *I Spy*. I never missed an episode. I wanted to revisit the gadgetry and stylishness of that genre but update it with '90s technology and sophistication. And, of course, what we never saw in those movies was what would happen if James Bond had to go home and answer to his family."

The other major theme in *True Lies* is relationships and commitment, also an aspect of the movie that Cameron is quite attached to. His Harry Tasker is a guy who pours everything, the best of himself, into his work for his country, then brings what is left over home to his wife and family. Cameron's contention was that a relationship simply cannot survive if you don't bring the best of yourself home. The echoes of his own marital problems are resoundingly obvious.

Marriage is something Cameron believes in but isn't very good at himself. Before the production of *True Lies* ended, the die would be cast for a third marriage. As for the schizophrenic nature of Cameron's own marriages, it's clear

that he is a passionate man who loves women but is so completely devoted to his work that his relationships come a
poor second.

When it came time to cast *True Lies*, Cameron had to work
around the lead role of Harry Tasker played by Arnold
Schwarzenegger. Schwarzenegger's presence in a film always
causes a ripple effect throughout the entire casting process:
actors have to be cast either with or against Arnold's
strengths and weaknesses. It was vital to cast Harry's wife,
Helen, with particular care.

Cameron had only one actress in mind for the role of
Helen, Jamie Lee Curtis. Curtis is a showbiz kid through
and through. Her father is Tony Curtis and her mother is
the legendary actress Janet Leigh. Jamie Lee began her
acting career as a teenager when she took a role in the television series *Operation Petticoat*. She made her movie debut
in the low-budget horror flick that would become one of
the most successful independent films ever made, John
Carpenter's *Halloween* (1978). She followed that with several starring roles in other B-grade horror movies with
titles like *Prom Night* and *Terror Train*, as well as starring in
the *Halloween* sequel, an interesting little Carpenter picture
called *The Fog*. In 1981 she snagged the starring female
role in the Paramount smash hit comedy *Trading Places*
opposite Eddie Murphy and Dan Aykroyd. She continued
to act in a wide variety of movies, some memorable, some

not, until landing what would be one of her best roles to date, the female lead in the riotously funny *A Fish Called Wanda* (1988). After scoring big in that British comedy Curtis decided to switch gears and take on a heavier role, that of the victimized policewoman in *Blue Steel,* an MGM movie produced by Oliver Stone and directed by Kathryn Bigelow.

Jamie Lee Curtis possessed just the right blend of toughness and feminine sexuality that Cameron was looking for in *True Lies.* It was on a visit to the *Blue Steel* set that he met Curtis, and this meeting led to Curtis being offered the role of Helen. It was also on this visit that James Cameron met and fell hard for the tall, exotically beautiful director Kathryn Bigelow, who became his wife in 1989.

Cameron needed to find the right actors to play the roles of Harry Tasker's sidekick and fellow secret agent, Gib, and the con-man who leads Harry's wife astray, Simon. Tom Arnold, best known as the husband of the volatile TV star Roseanne and as the star of his own sitcom, *The Jackie Thomas Show,* was contacted about playing Schwarzenegger's buddy. Arnold laughs when he recalls, "My agent called me up one day and asked me if I might be interested in doing a co-starring role in a James Cameron movie. I told him to stop kidding around and I hung up on him."

Eventually Tom Arnold was cast, and several reviewers declared that he walked away with the movie by being given all the best lines and making the most of them. For the role of the con-man Simon, Cameron went back to one of his favorite actors, Bill Paxton.

Actor Art Malik was chosen to play the terrorist leader Aziz in a manner that was quite unusual for a James Cameron movie. Cameron is adamant about auditioning actors for every role, without exception — but he made an exception for Art Malik. Cameron had been so impressed with Malik's performances in *The Living Daylights* and *City of Joy* that he offered Malik the role without an audition or even a reading. Malik then made a conscious effort to play Aziz straight, as a man with nothing to lose and everything to gain by committing terrorist acts. The political process has failed him and he sees himself as having nowhere else to turn. This portrayal later attracted criticism that had a negative impact on *True Lies'* box-office performance.

Cameron and his production team approached the United States Marine Corps for their support and were delighted when it was granted. The Marines even suggested that they could schedule a few training missions to coincide with the photographic needs of the movie. Even with that generous support it became evident that these sequences would need a lot of work. "No matter what, we had to establish convincingly that Arnold Schwarzenegger was actually flying the Harrier" is how John Bruno describes the huge but straightforward problem that faced the production.

Cameron wanted to have one close shot that showed

Schwarzenegger climbing into the cockpit of the jet, then in one continuous shot he wanted the camera to pull back to take in the Harrier lifting off the ground in a vertical takeoff. There was no way of achieving this aim other than by building a full-scale mock-up and stringing it up in the air somehow. Donald Pennington, a renowned model maker, was brought in to handle the job. Pennington had built the full-scale mock-ups for *The Abyss* and designed some of the custom-made props on *Terminator 2: Judgment Day*. A keen aircraft enthusiast, he was absolutely perfect for this gig.

The production team was invited to visit the Marine Corps Air Station at Yuma, Arizona, where key production heads were given the opportunity to study the AV-8B Harrier closely. Pennington determined that he needed to construct a fiberglass mold of the jet. The Marine Corps gave him permission to make the mold so long as he adhered to certain conditions. His crew of sixteen had a scant thirteen weeks in which to create the final model, so the need to complete the mold was urgent. "The Marines were great," says Pennington. "They actually towed the Harrier off the flight line into the hangar. We were allowed to go right to work. It was a huge break without which we would have had a whole different movie."

One of the main priorities was making sure that no harm at all came to the $23.5-million aircraft. Extra care had to be taken to make sure that the fiberglass didn't bond with the surface of the jet. The crew began by smearing a layer of polyester wax on the plane to keep the solvents and resins from eating through the surface of the aircraft. The wax would probably have been enough, but as an additional safety measure they smeared a polyvinyl alcohol under it all to guarantee a smooth release.

More than twenty-four separate molds would eventually be needed. Once it became clear that this mock-up idea might indeed work, John Bruno had to start looking at just how it would be used. "I went through Jim's storyboards and counted up eighty-five effects shots for the end sequence alone. That was a real budget-buster, so I started thinking of ways to cut it down a bit."

Meanwhile, location scouts scoured the Miami area for suitable sites and buildings. They came across a building that was so perfect for their needs that they couldn't believe their luck. The Intervera Building was a largely vacant twenty-story edifice right in the middle of the downtown business district. It had the right architectural design and featured an angular, mirrored surface. What made it a gift from above was a steel-reinforced housing on the roof that would be ideal for dramatic, downwardly aimed shots from any direction.

The Harrier jet still proved to be a problem. Whether they were using the film blue screen, a technique involving filming the mock-up Harrier against a blue screen and then adding in the background filmed elsewhere, or the digital green screen, whereby the image of the Harrier would be digitized by a computer program and then superimposed over footage shot on location, Cameron wanted as much motion as possible to lend credibility to the sequences. John Bruno remembers sitting and thinking, "Based on the shots we wanted and the amount of movement within them, I knew that we were going to need the biggest blue screen ever made, in conjunction with some wild boom and crane movements." But where would they put this huge blue screen? Months were spent searching for an area that was large enough. Finally they found the Synchro Aerodrome Business Center, a nearly vacant airplane hangar at the Van Nuys Airport.

The idea now was to put Schwarzenegger in the Harrier mock-up and move it around against the giant blue screen. That image would later be married to the image shot on top of the Intervera Building. A huge photographic image of downtown Miami shot panoramically from the roof of the building would also be needed for angles that could not be captured when shooting the scenes. As all this was being explained to James Cameron, he started picturing the scenario going one step further. He suggested that they could build a platform on the roof of the Intervera Building and put it on air disks so they could slide it back and forth while perched precariously atop the office tower. John Bruno says: "I made the offhanded remark that maybe we should build a whole motion-control rig right on top of the roof. Jim's eyes lit up and I knew we were in trouble."

Suddenly they went from playing around with a model jet in a hangar to putting Arnold Schwarzenegger 250 feet in the air in a gigantic machine with enough horsepower to push over an entire building. But herein lies the particular genius of James Cameron. He is not afraid of technology or machines. It is his feeling that if you get the best people available to work the machines there won't be any problem. The team's efforts now centered on building a powerful motion base coupled with a full-sized jet on top of an office building in the middle of Miami.

The aircraft mold was forty-seven feet long and had a thirty-foot wingspan, and it had to be enormously durable because it was going to be tossed around, hung on wires, and jumped on by the cast. Whenever possible during the construction of the mock-up, the team used real Harrier parts and components found at a Marine Corps maintenance depot in Cherry Point, North Carolina. Another lucky find was a cockpit that had been removed from a Harrier involved in a training accident. The acrylic canopy, the outrigger gear, and the rear main landing gear were also procured from the Marine depot.

No one knew what this extremely complex sequence would look like on film, or even if it could be set up so that Cameron could get the coverage that he needed. Once everything was in place on the roof, the first day of shooting proved to be the most trying. Mark Noel was in charge of overseeing the rooftop motion base and its operation and of constructing the propane gun that could simulate the Harrier's rapid-fire cannon by spewing eight-foot bursts of flame. Noel remembers: "We were on the roof the first day of shooting and they wanted Arnold in the cockpit. Jim wanted a big pitch and roll along with the firing of the gun. Now, that's all fine, everything was tightly controlled with safety wires, but I was asking myself, can't we do this on the sixth or seventh day when we've had time to work out some problems?"

Noel and his crew hadn't completely figured out how to lock the plane steadily into position, so they had to hold the jet down with their own hands and their own strength. Most of the motion-based moves were performed manually and in real time, but there were a few exceptions. In one scene the tail of the Harrier was supposed to hit a construction crane. Risking damage to either the Harrier mock-up or the construction crane was unthinkable, so the motion base was programmed to make a yawing move that had the Harrier mock-up draw right up to the crane but not actually touch it.

As usual on a movie project of this size, it was the little things overlooked by the besieged crew that would come back to haunt them. That was never more true than when the cockpit canopy of the Harrier was about to be shot to pieces with a full clip from an AK-47. Right off the bat it was clear that considerable license was going to be taken in this scene because the canopy on a fighter jet is made from three-quarter-inch Lexan; in other words, it is bulletproof. When camera tests were being done for another shot involving the Harrier, John Bruno discovered that the canopy was reflecting the stage lighting. Nothing worked to conceal the reflections, but something had to be done quickly, preferably before James Cameron heard anything about it. One solution was to shoot the scenes and then get the technicians at Digital Domain to erase the offending reflections with their computers — but this would cost millions of dollars, if it could be done at all. Cameron was told about the problem and calmly thought it out with John Bruno. They came up with a solution that was simple and without compromise: blow the canopy completely off in an earlier sequence and eliminate the problem altogether. Another scene involving blasting the canopy was devised as a back-up. The canopy was rigged with small explosives to imitate bullets smashing through the windshield. The idea was that the canopy would disintegrate like a windshield, but when the time came the Lexan proved to be a lot stronger than expected: not only was it bulletproof but it didn't disintegrate as planned. An exasperated James Cameron decided to go with having the canopy blown off early in the movie so the damn thing would never have to be dealt with again.

The filming of *True Lies* unrolled amidst one of the most oppressive heat waves in Florida's history, and rumors began to fly once again about Cameron's mistreatment of his crew.

Cameron had previously been regarded as tough, but now he was accused of being downright cruel. A frequently repeated rumor had Cameron not allowing anyone to go to the bathroom during working hours. He reportedly said that if you walked off the set to go to the bathroom, you could just keep right on walking because you were off the picture. Arnold Schwarzenegger was no exception to this rule. "I am suspended twenty, thirty stories up in the air and I have to go to the bathroom. Jim screams at me, 'No, you can't, you're now a military man on a mission. What if you were a real pilot and had to go on an attack mission, are you going to land to go to the bathroom?' Cameron would rather pee in his pants than leave the scene when things are clicking along."

To bolster their sagging morale and get their resentment across, several crew members had T-shirts made with the inscriptions "T-3 — Not for Me!" and "You Can't Scare Me — I Work for James Cameron."

One day a chief electrician approached Cameron to discuss a problem with rigging a complex scene. The electrician became so flustered that he snapped at Cameron, "There is probably a way to make this harder. You just haven't thought of it yet."

South Florida may summon up images of palm trees and soft breezes, but Cameron and his *True Lies* team experienced the true unpredictability of the region's weather, which slowed the shooting of *True Lies* to a snail's pace. Lightning-charged thunderstorms drifted in with regularity to threaten the safety of the cast and crew who were exposed on the office-tower rooftop. A special sensor was installed on the roof to provide a few minutes' warning of potential lightning strikes. On several occasions during the rooftop shoot, the sensor alarm sent the cast and crew scuttling to safety.

The crew were understandably nervous about the risks they were taking, as was Twentieth Century Fox, but for different reasons. The film was slated to cost $60 million. Fox saw that the weather was shredding the schedule, and Cameron was sensitive to their concerns. He started working out alternative schedules in the event that the carefully planned shots were ruined by the weather. Fox, still worried, turned Cameron down when he begged for more time to shoot on the rooftop. Cameron is not known as a profligate spender, but rather as a filmmaker who is scrupulous with money and puts every nickel on the screen. But studio executives are always happiest saying no, and they were haunted by the cautionary example of United Artists' failure to rein in filmmaker Michael Cimino during the *Heaven's Gate* fiasco. Cimino was given a budget of $12 million to make his 1980 western and he ran it up to almost $40 million. *Heaven's Gate* made less than $1 million at the box office and forced United Artists out of business. (The company was resurrected by MGM and is now back in business as MGM/UA.)

Cameron's brilliant solution to the problem of squeezing some more time into the rooftop shoot was to put
stuntmen on the Harrier while the crane was lifting it off
the roof and lowering it to the ground. Cameras were
hung off the side of the building and another angle was
covered by a hovering helicopter. In so doing he saved himself six or seven complicated composite shots that would
have made even more costly blue screen work necessary.
John Bruno provides more details. "Jim managed to squeeze
one more day out of the rooftop shoot by doing that. It
was a wild scene. Right after we finished on the roof, the
Harrier was lifted off the motion base and lowered onto
the street, where the stunt people climbed on and were
safety-cabled to it. Then it was hoisted about two hundred
feet off the ground. Jim was shooting from a helicopter
while I was up on the roof with a VistaVision camera and
there was another camera across the street on the Capital
Band building."

The stunt people included Kim Zimmerman, a tiny
woman with a circus background who doubled Eliza
Dushku, who was playing Harry Tasker's daughter; Billy
Lucas doubling Arnold Schwarzenegger, and Jimmy Roberts
doubling Art Malik. The scene consisted of thirty minutes
of action starting with Roberts jumping onto the back of
the plane and crawling his way up to the cockpit to attack
Lucas with a knife. Zimmerman was hanging off the nose
of the Harrier while Lucas was trying to grab her and pull

her up. When Cameron saw how much fun the stunt people were having he invented a new twist: he suggested that the fight be done while the jet was spinning. The stunt people responded with a unanimous "Go ahead, spin us!"

There were several times during the making of the movie that Arnold Schwarzenegger himself was caught a little *too* close to the action. In one sequence he has commandeered a horse and chases the bad guys through the streets, then into a Miami hotel, into the elevator, and onto the roof. Schwarzenegger remembers the scene from the safe vantage point of hindsight: "In that scene on the rooftop of the hotel the horse freaked out and almost stepped, literally, over the rooftop. If he had taken one step further we would have fallen thirty feet to the ground."

Often, though, a stunt in a movie is like a magic trick: once the mechanics of the trick are explained to you, once the veneer of the trick is off, then you tell yourself that there really isn't much to it. One stunt during the bridge sequence fits firmly into this category. A helicopter hovers over the limo carrying Jamie Lee Curtis. A rope ladder is lowered and Curtis grabs it through the sunroof. She is lifted out through the sunroof just before the limo plunges off the wrecked bridge into the water. Cameron explains that the trick to that scene is that Curtis was never in the car at all. "She was attached to the helicopter and the helicopter flew up and matched the speed of the car. She was lowered down into the car [and the film was reversed]. So no matter what it looked like there was never any way she could have gone over the edge with the car."

Once the Miami shooting was completed, the company headed to the Keys to film the scenes that involved Harry Tasker and his wife being held hostage by the Crimson Jihad and their escape from captivity. The escape included a Harrier attack on the truck carrying atomic weapons, the most visually stunning sequence in the whole movie.

The sequence was shot on a section of the Seven Mile Bridge that was decommissioned in 1982 when a more functional bridge was completed beside it. A span of the bridge that was once used as a turngate for ships had been removed, providing Cameron with exactly what he needed. They could dress that section in a way to make it look like it had just been blown apart, which would allow the limousine in the sequence previously described to drive off and plunge into the water. During a location scouting trip to Miami the scouts found a spot on the Miami River where an entire bridge had been dismantled. The production was able to rent the remains of the bridge to be used as wreckage. The pieces were loaded onto barges and floated to the shooting location in the Keys. The pieces were arranged around the bridge, then sunk. The sequence was shot and the junk was floated back up to its original spot.

Part of this sequence involved the Harrier jets blasting apart a large section of the bridge. Real Harriers had flown over the Seven Mile Bridge in a mock attack, but it was up to Digital Domain to provide the realism. It quickly became clear that a large model of the bridge would be required, and the question of where this model would be constructed loomed large. John Bruno relates, "We actually considered several alternatives. There was the tank at Universal, but that wouldn't have been big enough. There was the Sultan Sea, where we shot some stuff on *The Abyss*. But there was something about the Florida Keys — the lighting, the sky, the water — that would have been impossible for us to duplicate anywhere else. Plus, the water was shallow there and there were no waves, which made it great for maintaining scale in miniature."

Getting permits to shoot in the Florida Keys was a bureaucratic nightmare. Rumors had been going around that Cameron was heading to Florida to make a huge action picture that involved blowing up the causeway. The company spent several days with the state environmental officials looking for a suitable place to stage their explosions. Even places that looked feasible came with many restrictions. The State of Florida did not want *True Lies* even working in areas that contained fragile life forms like sponges or coral heads or turtle grass, much less setting off huge explosions. Finally Cameron received permission to shoot in a section of the isolated Sugarloaf Key.

Pat McLurg was hired to supervise building the bridge model. McLurg had worked with Cameron on both *Aliens* and *The Abyss*, so he knew going in that the only thing he could expect was the unexpected. He was asked to build a five-span miniature of the Seven Mile Bridge. The model would be one-fifth scale, which would make it nearly two hundred feet long, with eighty feet being a fully detailed rendering. The rest of the structure would consist of scaffolding that needed to be strong enough to support the tracks that the model truck was to travel on.

The bridge model turned out beautifully, but there remained the question of what it should look like after it was blown up. Small tabletop versions of the model were made so McLurg and Cameron could determine how the pieces were to fall. Cameron was fixated on recreating the infamous "luckiest man in Baghdad" footage shot during the Gulf War. In that incident, a truck is seen driving across a bridge seconds before it is vaporized by American ordnance. Cameron loved the look of pure destructive power without a lot of flame.

By early December everything was ready to go. One last detail needed to be addressed — the truck. The truck carrying the terrorists was still in perfect condition because the chase scene leading up to the bridge scene had yet to be shot. The four-foot-long model of the truck and drivers was taken to Marathon, Florida, where Cameron was directing the first unit. He loved the model truck but wondered how to make it look as if it had been through a crash. When Cameron was told that the model was made of lead, he smiled, asked for a hammer, and started whacking away at the front end to achieve the desired effect.

Following a week of picture-perfect weather, the day arrived to shoot the big bridge, but filming had to be postponed for a day because of gray skies and gusting winds that caused white-capped waves that would throw the scale of the model bridge way out of sync. The next day everything was set up and ready to go, but before the big explosion could be detonated state environmental representatives were sent up in an ultralight aircraft to search for any turtles or manatee in the area.

Once the bridge was finally exploded Cameron was satisfied with what he had seen, but he organized a second take just for insurance. It took the crew only two days to carefully reconstruct the bridge; everyone knew that after this second take not enough raw material would be left to reconstruct it for a third take. Cameron had watched the first take on videotape but he was on the scene for the second one. To everyone's surprise he was calm and cool. He checked every camera angle and then stepped back and said he was going to watch the proceedings with everyone else.

Take two went off nearly perfectly. John Bruno remembers, "The second explosion went off and big chunks of the bridge were splashing into the water and there was lingering dust in the air. And there was no scale problem at all. It's as realistic an explosion on water as I have ever seen."

James Cameron believes in giving credit where it is

due. "Credit for the final look of that sequence has to go to John Bruno. He urged me to shoot in Florida so that the water would match, the sky would match, and the color would match. We also had the original bridge right nearby for reference. We just went with a big-assed model and blew it out of the water.

"At one point we'd considered doing the explosion full sized by spanning the gap of the Seven Mile Bridge then actually blowing it up. In fact, that idea was shared by quite a few people once it became generally known how expensive the model was going to be. It was thought that it would actually be cheaper to build a real bridge and blow it up, but it would have to be made of balsa wood and other breakaway materials that would look really fake flying through the air."

Back in Los Angeles the work at the Van Nuys airplane hangar was about to go full tilt. But in the early-morning hours of January 17, 1993, the Northridge earthquake hit. It had a magnitude of 6.7 on the Richter scale and the epicenter was one mile from the Van Nuys airport. The crew went to work the next day expecting the very worst but were stunned to find only minimal damage. The hangar had to be inspected and a few essential repairs had to be done before the production could resume, but only three days were lost.

The final scene of *True Lies* features a big visual joke when Harry and Helen Tasker embrace blissfully against the

beautiful southern Florida sky while an atomic bomb detonates in the background without their noticing. Computer
animator Jamie Dixon was assigned the job of simulating the
blast. In 1989 he had done the simulation of the first atomic
explosion test for the Roland Joffe movie *Fat Man and Little
Boy*. Coincidentally, Dixon's father, a physical chemist, had
been involved in the Manhattan Project at Los Alamos
and played a role in the development of the real atom bomb.

James Cameron's fear of atomic war has been constant
throughout his life and his career. It has found its way into
each and every movie with the exception of *Piranha 2* and
Titanic. Cameron is very conscious of this thematic thread.
"I suppose you could draw the conclusion that I think a lot
about nuclear war," he admits. "It's something I have edu-
cated myself quite extensively on. While studying physics
in college I got a pretty good understanding of what goes
on from a physics standpoint. It's the moral perspective
that I am still trying to wrap my head around. The fact
that of all the nations on earth with nuclear capability the
United States is the only country to have actually used
atomic weapons on a human target. And the idea that all
that stuff is still out there, and that the world is in this
collective denial. It's amazing."

There is something oddly out of place, in a comedy,
about having a terrorist group detonating a nuclear weapon
over American soil to show the United States government that they mean business, but James Cameron was

completely unfazed by the criticism. "I wanted to push some buttons with that scene," he explains, "to see what kind of reaction I got. It was supposed to be like the fireworks out the window the moment Cary Grant and Grace Kelly embrace in Hitchcock's *To Catch a Thief* — only on a somewhat larger scale. Some people will find it inappropriate for a comedy. But not if you take the whole movie very lightly, and appreciate its outrageous tone and the fact that it is really a marital fable. The idea that Helen is so in love with Harry that she doesn't notice a nuclear explosion while they are kissing is really pretty funny. At least *I* think it is."

While Cameron was expressing his subconscious angst and trying to break out of his sci-fi mold he was also spending a ton of money. A movie that was budgeted at $60 million was now crossing the $100-million mark. Fox was fretful but sufficiently impressed with what they were seeing of the film in production to feel confident of having a worldwide hit on their hands, in which case it would be money well spent. The bottom line was that Arnold Schwarzenegger's name on a movie pretty well guaranteed that it would be sold into just about every market on earth and quickly earn back the studio's investment.

True Lies opened with a solid but not spectacular weekend take of $25.5 million. It then slipped steadily as each week went by. The final domestic take was $149 million, impressive if not for the fact that the movie finally cost an estimated

$120 million to make, Cameron's second record-setting outing. The hit movie that summer of 1994 was *Forrest Gump*, with Disney's *The Lion King* also bringing in big dollars at the box office.

Public and critical reaction to *True Lies* was negative the second it hit the screens. M. T. Mehdi, head of the National Council on Islamic Affairs, protested to Twentieth Century Fox about the film's plot and called for a boycott of the movie. Mehdi was worried that the movie would increase prejudice against Arabs and Islam. He claimed that he received ten thousand letters and thousands of phone calls from outraged viewers after the film opened. In Washington, pickets gathered around theaters showing the film and paraded up and down the sidewalks with signs reading "Open Your Eyes and Terminate the Lies" and "Hasta la Vista Fairness." In response Twentieth Century Fox attached a disclaimer to the end credits that read "This film is a work of fiction and does not represent the action or beliefs of a particular culture or religion."

There were also loud accusations of misogyny. Jamie Lee Curtis is caught in a compromising position with Simon the con-man and is then forced to perform a humiliating striptease in front of her husband, Harry, who is concealed behind a two-way mirror. Cameron stayed silent on this issue because to explain himself one way or the other would only draw more attention to criticism that he believed to be nonsense. Arnold Schwarzenegger was a bit more vocal. "This scene, the whole movie, has to be taken lightly, because that's the way that it was made," instructed the actor. While in London promoting the movie Schwarzenegger was asked whether he perceived this scene to be demeaning to women. His reply: "I let my wife strip for me too. I don't know what kind of household you have, how kinky you get in your house, but I think those kinds of things keep a marriage alive."

Most reviewers were taken in by the visual razzle-dazzle of *True Lies* but weren't impressed with the story. *Daily Variety* called the film "141 minutes of an enticing three-minute trailer." *Time*, which had been one of Cameron's champions in the early days, was harsh with the latest effort. They pronounced the movie "a loud misfire." But they did think, mistakenly, that audiences would turn out in droves to "enjoy the lavish squandering of talent by Hollywood's shrewdest showman."

Cameron was disappointed at the reception but was energized and delighted by the work done by Digital Domain. He was proud that his little company had supplied the most realistic simulation of a jet engine's back blast that had ever been put on film. He saw great things ahead for Digital Domain and would spend the next few years developing the company while incubating several movie projects, including an epic historical romance entitled *Titanic*.

Ten

SURFING THE NEXT WAVE: DIGITAL DOMAIN AND *T2 3-D*

"There was something happening that I don't think anyone could either push forward or hold back."

JAMES CAMERON

James Cameron and his partners Stan Winston and Scott Ross launched their solid-state effects house, Digital Domain, in 1992. The company was quickly formed to do the effects work for Cameron's *True Lies* but then rapidly branched out into servicing other feature projects, video games, CD-ROMs, and TV commercials. Currently Digital Domain has a staff of more than eighty digital artists, eighteen software developers, seven systems administrators, eight technical assistants, and several computer graphics operators, model makers, producers, and coordinators. They are considered one of the finest visual effects teams in the world, after only five years of operation. By the end of 1997 the staff is projected to number over five hundred. Digital Domain has already been nominated for two Oscars and has won sixteen awards in other media.

With firm corporate backing from IBM, Digital Domain has started making serious strides toward becoming an actual studio. In February of 1996 the company took on another full partner in Cox Enterprises, a leading media company that is developing the most technologically advanced broadband cable systems. Jim Kennedy, chairman and CEO of Cox Enterprises, says he was delighted to get involved with Cameron, Winston, Ross, and Digital Domain because of their audacity and ambition. This partnership allows Digital Domain to accelerate their schedule for investments in research and development, facilities, technology, and personnel.

There are many who credit James Cameron with pioneering the next wave of the evolution of cinematic technology. Cameron accepts some of the credit (or blame) for the technological turn the movies are taking, but he won't take it all. "I was lucky enough to be surfing the wave when it first broke. There was something happening that I don't think anyone could either push forward or hold back.

There was an opportunity to ride the wave at exactly the right time. We took that opportunity on *The Abyss*, we took it again on *Terminator 2: Judgment Day*, and we took it a third time with Digital Domain. But before I became involved in computer graphics, there was a good ten or fifteen years of pioneering work with people writing the code necessary to do the 3-D imaging and figuring out how to do the polygonal modeling and early inverse kinematics. It was all being done but it was being done in rarefied environments, in universities and R&D labs of the big software companies. It hadn't reached the artists per se. It hadn't cross-pollinated into the film industry, which had both the art and the money to make it a real cultural phenomenon. But everybody wanted it to happen, everybody had been trying."

Cameron goes on to say, "There were fledgling efforts in films like *Tron* and *The Last Starfighter*. There was even a bit of liquid-metal morphing in a movie called *The Navigator*. It was composited optically, not digitally, and it was done in a kind of crude manner but it was effective. From a filmmaker's perspective, though, I was pioneering. I took a leap of faith on *The Abyss* and I took an even greater leap on *T2*, because on *The Abyss* the computer was brought in to solve a single sequence, and if the sequence had failed the film still would have worked dramatically. On *T2* the success or failure of the film was really predicated on the success or failure of the digital effects techniques.

"The great leap of faith was that we were ready to, or could, risk a $90-million negative, which is a pretty high investment, on a group of people at ILM who couldn't guarantee that they could do what I wanted them to do. But they said, 'We think we are ready.' "

One of Cameron's goals in conceiving Digital Domain was to make the interface between the filmmakers and technology easier to arrange and more cost-effective. Today anything is possible if you have the money. The tools exist, either on their own or in combinations. Cameron's aim over the next ten years is to give unity to all these disparate tools. He believes that the next hurdle to be jumped will be the creation of either a fully animated computer-generated movie character that is photorealistic, or a feature that contains a significant amount of photorealistic animation.

So far even the most ambitious computer-generated projects, like *Jurassic Park*, limit the use of these computer-generated images. Such images in *Jurassic Park* add up to only five or six minutes in total screen time. *Toy Story* took another step forward, but the combination of cartoon-like art direction and photorealistic renderings gave the film its intended surreal quality. With *T2* Cameron blended digital imagery seamlessly into the weave of the film, bring-ing it up to the point where viewers can't tell where the live action stops and the computer-generated images begin.

Digital Domain was nominated for Academy Awards in the Best Visual Effects category first for their pioneering work in *True Lies* and then for the spectacular work done for Ron Howard on *Apollo 13* (1995). In fact Howard was hesitant to go ahead with *Apollo 13* until Digital Domain was officially on board. *Chain Reaction,* the controversial *Island of Dr. Moreau,* and Luc Besson's dazzling $95-million science fiction epic *The Fifth Element* have all recently used Digital Domain for their effects. Digital Domain also won a Grammy Award for their work on the Rolling Stones video *Love Is Strong.*

Partner Scott Ross contends that the ultimate goal of Digital Domain is to become a full-fledged studio like Disney or Paramount. Ross has a healthy sense of the competition between Digital Domain and Industrial Light & Magic, which he more or less ran from 1988 to 1992. He was senior vice-president of LucasArts and was responsible for bringing digital technology to ILM. He would like to see Digital Domain eclipse what ILM is doing. "We want to develop digital characters, digital content, and a digital environment and deliver it to our audience through a digital medium to the home or office."

Digital Domain is working hard on something they call "performance capture." This is a process of capturing, through computer animation, the very essence of a character and a performance — making the animated character seem real right down to the furrowing of a brow or the narrowing of the eyes in a certain expression. Performance capture was put to use on John Frankenheimer's *The Island*

of Dr. Moreau and will be used again by Stan Winston when
he applies the process to the new Michael Jackson musical
short film that he will direct.

One of the first people DD hired as a computer animation artist was Kevin Mack, a one-time bodybuilder
who has had a lifelong fascination with human anatomy.
Soon after, he launched HARD, which stands for Human
Animation Research and Development. Working with a
set of digital "bones," Mack sets out to play God, making
and attaching muscles to the skeleton one at a time until
he duplicates the entire scheme of human musculature.
Once that is accomplished he goes on to create the skin
and the hair. This is a major step toward creating the first
photorealistic computer-generated actor. Mack's work is
being incorporated into the ambitious project Cameron
has planned as the next movie he makes after *Titanic*, to be
called *Avatar*, in which the "stars" of the movie will be six
fully photorealistic computer-generated actors. No one has
a clue how this highly experimental process will evolve,
but the Screen Actors Guild has little to fear in the short
run. Scott Ross is the first to admit that "this stuff is really
expensive. Arnold Schwarzenegger is expensive, but it is
still cheaper to use the real thing than a computer to ani-
mate him. But in an area where we need Arnold to do
something he isn't capable of doing, then computer animation makes sense. If you do this just as a gimmick then it
simply won't work."

One of the fastest-growing divisions of Digital Domain is the new-media department headed by Steve Schklair, which went from one employee to fifty-five in just one year. This division focuses on video games. The hottest trend in games today is multiplayer online networks. Digital Domain is developing games for Internet surfers, but they won't release these games until a wider bandwidth becomes available. With current bandwidth capabilities, images for online games don't transmit as quickly as they should for a completely immersive gaming experience. Schklair believes that "since Digital Domain stands for quality, the production of the games must be as high as our movies or they are not ready to be released."

The first two games out of the gate are *Ted Shred* and *Book of Virtues*. *Ted Shred* takes its players to the furthest edge of skateboarding, kayaking, and surfing and involves a group of evildoers trying to seize a beautiful tropical island for themselves. Ted Shred, the coolest, most radical surfer ever, stands in their way. Players assume the role of Ted Shred and battle their opponents to win back the island.

Book of Virtues in an interactive CD-ROM series for children that explores stories from history and literature. The series aims to engage parents as participants in the program by offering them ways to extend and personalize the impact of the stories on their children.

Digital Domain offers employees the chance to do exciting cutting-edge work and share in the generous stock

option opportunities. The employees repay the company
with their enthusiasm. Steve Schklair describes how "people just hang around here after work. Sometimes they work
so late I literally have to tell them to go home."

Perhaps the most interesting and most spectacular project
that Digital Domain has been involved in to date is the
amusement park attraction *T2 3-D Battle Across Time*, a
twelve-minute sequel to *Terminator 2: Judgment Day* that
was in development for a full four years. Cameron considers *T2 3-D* the legitimate third chapter in the *Terminator*
series even though it is so short and can be seen in only
one venue. He hasn't ruled out another feature film involving the Terminator, and a further sequel is in the early-
planning stage.

Universal Pictures approached Gary Goddard, president
of Landmark Entertainment, about the idea in the fall of
1992. Landmark Entertainment are experts in theme park
design and have designed several movie-based attractions
in the past (*Kongfrontation, Jaws, Ghostbusters,* and *Conan*).
Goddard and his chief designer, Adam Bezark, watched *T2*
over and over again trying to come up with a suitable angle
to use for their purposes. The idea of using live actors on a
stage as part of the presentation was discussed. They then had
to go through the process of getting the approval of Carolco
Pictures, producer Gale Anne Hurd, and James Cameron.

In December 1992 Goddard and Bezark presented

Cameron with a thirty-page treatment, detailed storyboards, and hundreds of color sketches and designs. Cameron liked the idea but decided that if he was to be involved it would have to unfold in a very specific way. "My initial contribution was to sell Universal on the idea that we needed the actual cast and not just a bunch of generic actors. They suggested that the Terminator have his face pretty much blown off, meaning that it wouldn't matter if it was Arnold Schwarzenegger. But I couldn't see how that would work. I pointed out that this was an attraction that was going to appeal to six-year-olds, who probably didn't want to see a bloody ripped-off face like in the two R-rated films it was predicated on."

Cameron reworked the dialogue and pared down the effects. Over the next twelve months, *T2 3-D* remained in development because talks were continuing with Cameron, his Lightstorm Entertainment, and Digital Domain. In March 1995, after nearly three years of discussion, development, and tests, Universal finally gave the project the go-ahead. Cameron set the record for most expensive movie ever made with *T2*, then broke his own record with *True Lies.* In 1995 Kevin Reynolds's *Waterworld* took that distinction away from him, but it can be argued that with *T2 3-D Battle Across Time* he has taken the title back. The short movie cost just over $60 million to make. At that rate of spending, had it been made into a full-length feature it would have surpassed $200 million.

Cameron succeeded in persuading Arnold Schwarze-negger to reprise his role for a third time, along with Linda Hamilton, Eddie Furlong, and Robert Patrick. Everyone came back without having to be urged in the slightest. Cameron also wanted to shoot the picture in super-high-quality 65-mm format and in 3-D. "We wanted to do some-thing spectacular and there is an enhanced sense of reality that comes from the high-resolution 65-mm film format we chose, mixed with the illusion of depth offered by 3-D. Combine this with the live action stuff and it's really quite effective and very immense."

T2 3-D is projected onto three screens each measuring twenty-three by fifty feet, and the sound comes out of 159 speakers. It makes for an unforgettable amusement park experience.

Cameron decided to split up the directing duties for the sake of time and to maximize the creativity of all involved. Stan Winston and John Bruno were brought in as co-directors. Cameron directed the actors, Winston directed the sequences requiring robots, and Bruno directed the pyrotechnics. Cameron hired his longtime friend Chuck Comisky as overall producer and visual effects supervisor. Comisky had given Cameron his first paying job on a movie when he hired him to work on *Battle Beyond the Stars* at Corman's New World Pictures fifteen years earlier.

Act one of *T2 3-D* begins in the present at Universal Studios, Florida, where the Cyberdyne Corporation has

ostensibly assembled the audience for the unveiling of its latest technological innovation, the Cyberdyne Systems model
T-70 automatic fighting infantry unit. The audience is
instructed to don their safety (3-D) glasses for protection
from the chromed eight-foot-tall animatronic T-70's laser
fire. The presentation is interrupted when stunt actors playing John and Sarah Connor rappel into the theater with
guns blazing, spoiling Cyberdyne's special technological
event. Alarm sirens blare and emergency lights flash as bullets blast through the Cyberdyne lab that covers the entire
wall behind the stage. With a strange metallic sucking sound
the bullet holes heal themselves and the logo melts into
the liquid-metal malevolence known as the T-1000, which
shoots out into the audience and appraises its enemies, John
and Sarah Connor. Suddenly, with a blinding flash of light,
a time sphere appears, out of which the Terminator roars
onto the stage on his customary Fatboy Harley-Davidson.

The Terminator grabs John Connor and leaps back
through the glowing time portal. This places the audience
in act two, the seven-minute, 65-mm, 3-D cinematic chase
through a post-apocalyptic Los Angeles in the year 2029,
where the T-1000 is joined by a massive flying Hunter-
Killer in hot pursuit. Act three has the Terminator and
John Connor descending into the bowels of the colossal
Cyberdyne Skynet headquarters, intent on destroying
the nerve center of the corporation, the heavily guarded
mainframe computer network.

For James Cameron the experience of making *T2 3-D* was a step forward. "*T2 3-D* is a blend of the science fiction that I know taken to a new extreme. We're integrating film and the proscenium theatrical experience into the same project. We have characters actually jumping in and out of the screen, so we are breaking down the barrier between the audience and the events in the picture. It wasn't until we started doing 3-D testing at Digital Domain that I realized just how fantastic this project could really be."

Because this was a multimedia event, Cameron brought in several crew members who were tops in their fields. Russell Carpenter, his *True Lies* director of photography, was hired to handle the live action photography. Peter Anderson, a top 3-D cinematographer, was brought on board to handle the three-dimensional photography, while Russell Lyster directed the green screen miniature shots.

To pull off this undertaking, several technologies that aren't thought of as being compatible had to be made so. Film, theatrical presentation, and special venue/simulation ride entertainment had to be married in a way that had never been attempted before. Stepping off the cliff into that kind of unknown territory is what Cameron excels at: "We looked at all the attractions at all the theme parks just to see how things were done. Then we specifically focused on anything with 3-D in it — of which there were a number of predecessors — and we analyzed what sorts of shots worked and what the effective moments were. We then tried to integrate that into the design of our show so we could optimize that format."

At their most rudimentary 3-D effects are difficult to pull off, but the level of realism that Cameron was insisting on required technology and techniques that were the latest yet devised. On a platform base two cameras were mounted, one horizontally and one vertically, both shot into a 50/50 beam-splitter mirror. To create the 3-D effect, each camera represents the slightly different perspectives that the right and left eye would normally use to perceive depth. The beam splitter enables the camera's lenses to see virtually the same image, but with an interocular distance between them analogous to the distance between human eyes, but taking into account the fifty-foot theater screen's image magnification. The angle at which the lenses are aimed into the mirror establishes the spatial distance from the screen that the object appears to the eye, or the distance at which the eyes converge on the object. These various factors determine how the brain interprets three-dimensional images.

Five separate 3-D camera rigs, weighing almost four hundred pounds each, were used during the production of *T2 3-D Battle Across Time* — at times, three of the 65-mm rigs were rolling simultaneously.

The movie's dynamic opening sequence through the debris-strewn war zone had to match the ferocious, kinetic scenes from the first two movies shot by Adam Greenberg, and they contain even more dazzling and exciting feats.

The crew had intended to return to the disused Kaiser Street Mill in Fontana, California, where they had shot the first and second *Terminator* movies, but by the time they were gearing up to shoot this installment they discovered that the plant had been taken apart bit by bit and shipped to China. They ended up filming in an open-pit mine near Eagle Mountain, California. This location filming was scheduled to last two weeks in mid-May because this was the only time Arnold Schwarzenegger, James Cameron, Linda Hamilton, and Eddie Furlong were all available.

Filming at the Eagle Mountain site included an action sequence that had Schwarzenegger and Furlong fleeing a Hunter-Killer that is firing repeatedly at them. Several multistory structures constructed for the movie were blown up one after another, creating a sequential, quarter-mile-long explosion.

When filming wrapped at Eagle Mountain the production moved to a studio facility in Hollywood where more control over lighting and logistics could be gained.

T2 3-D Battle Across Time achieved something quite remarkable. It put the audience *in* a James Cameron movie. Audiences don't just watch this movie, it is all around them.

Cameron had pushed cinema ahead once again and he took great pleasure in doing so. "We decided that you could take something very hard-edged from the feature film environment, soften the edges, put it in a themed attraction, and still keep what's fun and kinetic about it. Most of the

3-D movies that I have seen have maybe two shots that are memorable for having great 3-D; neither of them were images where something slammed you in the face. My philosophy was that we could have shot this movie in 35-mm 2-D, and with the cast and story we had, people would still go and see it. Everything else was just a big bonus."

Eleven

TITANIC

BIG DREAMS, BIGGER RISKS, BIGGEST SUCCESS: JAMES CAMERON AND THE ART OF HOLLYWOOD BRINKMANSHIP

"It's a metaphor for the inevitability of death.
We're all on the Titanic.*"*

JAMES CAMERON

Titanic *sailed on April 10, 1912. But in May 1898, a novel titled* Futility *described a British liner called* Titan, *which hit an iceberg in the North Atlantic and sank on her maiden voyage without enough lifeboats on board.*

The most commonly traded currency in Hollywood isn't money — it's dreams. For those who have them, dreams are the keys to the kingdom. For five long years, James Cameron dreamt about making a grand historical romance, set against the backdrop of the world's greatest marine disaster — the sinking of the fabled luxury liner *Titanic*.

Cameron's decision to go ahead with an epic movie on a subject that has been written about and filmed numerous times before was met with a degree of skepticism. But Cameron was nonplussed. If anything, he was more defiant and more confident. His film completed, Cameron commented on this issue: "A lot of wags and detractors were saying the ending of the film would be common knowledge and that [it] lessened the dramatic impact of the story. I take the opposite view. If my characters can draw you into the story, the love story, then everything that you know is coming, the inevitable horrors that you know await these people, make the movie all the more effecting and poignant because you know these feelings they are having have only a short time to flourish."

He had a point. These events have been told cinematically a number of times before, and on each of those occasions, there was a reasonable expectation that the audiences knew the fate of the ship and her passengers.

In 1953, Twentieth Century Fox released *Titanic*, starring Barbara Stanwyck and Clifton Webb. It was a highly dramatic, 97-minute film that was very effective in capturing both the majesty of the ship, the pomp and ceremony of the first-class passengers, and the drama and barely fathomable human tragedy of the disaster. The movie was directed by Jean Negulesco and produced and co-written by frequent Billy Wilder collaborator Charles Brackett. It won an Academy Award in 1953 for Best Screenplay and Best Story.

In 1955, writer Walter Lord published what has to be considered one of the most compelling accounts of the tragedy in his book *A Night to Remember* (Bantam Books, 1955). Lord told the story with economy, in 149 pages. He began his yarn with the mighty ship hitting the iceberg, taking us through the harrowing hours as the ship sank, then described the situation for those in the lifeboats. He concluded the story with some interesting social commentary about the role class played in the tragedy and the ensuing public reaction. The book contained dialogue taken from letters and diaries, and testimony from survivors, weaving through the events like a tautly-paced novel. In the closing pages, Lord listed the people who sailed on *Titanic*; the names in italics signified those who were rescued. According to sources at Bantam Books, *A Night to Remember* has sold over 500,000 copies in North America since the beginning of 1998. Two years after the release of Lord's book, the British production company Rank Organization bought the film rights. It was turned over to the excellent mystery novelist Eric Ambler to adapt into a screenplay. The result, directed by Roy Baker, was a 123-minute, near masterpiece of gut-wrenching, heartstring-tugging moviemaking. Director Baker, in a stroke of chilling brilliance, began his film with actual, grainy footage of the *Titanic* leaving port in Southampton. The viewer experienced the tragic events in a tremendously moving manner through the eyes of Second Officer Lightoller (beautifully played by Kenneth More). Until Cameron's film, this version was the *Titanic* movie of record in that those who had seen the movie described it as nothing short of brilliant and completely emotionally involving.

As Cameron was toiling away on his film, another incarnation of the *Titanic* story surfaced — this time, on Broadway, as a piece of musical theater. Expensive, bold, and lavish, this musical was written by Peter Stone (story and book) and Maury Yeston (music and lyrics) and was directed by Richard Jones. Because of the elaborate sets, the show went through some difficult times during previews. On at least one occasion, the story would play itself out only to be let down when the hydraulic rig, which was supposed to sink the set, failed. Once the bugs were worked out and the show hit the Lunt-Fontanne Theater, it was hailed as spectacular. Sheridan Morley wrote in *The London Spectator*, "The greatest American musical to have been written in fifteen years. A triumph! A score which soars ... a masterpiece." Nancy Franklin of *The New Yorker* raved: "Astonishingly, it manages to be grave and entertaining, somber and joyful. Little by little, you realize that you are in the presence of a genuine addition to American musical theater." When it came time to give out the 1997 Tony Awards, *Titanic* won five awards including Best Musical (as well as Best Book, Best Score, Best Sets and Best Orchestration).

It seems that James Cameron's feelings were accurate in that the general public has an endless fascination for the drama that unfolded that night in the North Atlantic. Particularly, anyone who gives any thought to the tragedy will ask himself or herself the endlessly compelling question: "What would I have done if I were there?"

It is early July 1996 in Halifax, Nova Scotia. The modern-day sequences of Cameron's script were to be shot in Halifax due to its proximity to the actual resting place of the great liner. Production of principal photography on what will turn out to be the biggest motion picture in history commences quietly. There is no hint of the gargantuan proportions this film would assume, but the storm clouds gathered early. July 2, 1997 was to be the release date of the film.

The complexity of making a film about the *Titanic* became evident immediately on the Halifax set. Cameron hired the Russian research vessel *Akademik Mistislav Keldysh* and its full crew as well as two high-tech, deep-water submersibles known as Mirs. These Russian vessels were to provide the backdrop for the present-day portions of the story involving treasure hunter Brock Lovett and his search for a valuable necklace — *le coeur de la mer* (heart of the ocean) — lost when *Titanic* sank. There are only four Mirs in the world, and the studios had to post a $25-million insurance bond on each of the two that Cameron was using. The submersibles are extremely sensitive. Nothing sharp could be worn near them — no belts, no walkie-talkies, and no glasses. If the thin seals around the hatches were even slightly scratched, the craft would be rendered unusable.

As is his reputation, even though it would be questioned vehemently throughout production, Cameron was maniacally cognizant of safety procedures. Since helicopters were being used daily, Cameron made sure the pilots knew their landing zones, their secondary landing zones if fuel ran out, and where to ditch safely in case of emergency. Because the cast and crew were working on the water and on a sea-bound vessel, Cameron insisted that numerous mandatory man-overboard drills were practised.

However, even though this was a $100-million-plus production, it wasn't without its moments of levity. Early on in the pre-production period leading up to the Halifax shoot, Cameron discovered a Canadian delicacy known as the Crunchie bar, a confection that consisted of golden sponge toffee wrapped in milk chocolate. Cameron developed a craving for the candy bars, but he found that more than one a day wired him up more than was good for him — or anyone close by. A production assistant (PA) was hired with the exclusive job description of seeing to it that Cameron was rationed only one Crunchie bar daily. One day, the hapless assistant fell down on the job. Cameron got his hands on *four* Crunchies and ate them in rapid succession, rendering him a holy terror for the next several hours. The PA was scolded severely by Kristie Sills, the first assistant director who had hired him. On another day,

Sills was showing a colleague some photos from her home-
town of Niagara Falls, Ontario. Cameron sauntered by and
looking over her shoulder, commented, "That's Niagara
Falls. That's where I'm from." Sills replied that she knew this
and that they went to the same high school — Stamford
Collegiate. Cameron then enthusiastically recounted how a
theater complex at Stamford had been named after him. Here
is the man with his hand on the throttle of one of the most
monstrous movie projects in history taking time to tell high-
school stories to his crew.

Ten days were originally scheduled for the Halifax leg of
the shoot. That stretched into forty days and forty nights. And
in almost biblical fashion, all hell broke loose on the final
night of the shoot.

It had been a long and physically grueling time, and the cast
and crew was about to take a break before heading to Rosarito
Beach, Mexico, where the balance of the film was to be shot. An
air of celebration surrounded these last few hours in Halifax,
and Cameron decided to eat with his cast and crew instead of
alone in his office as he had done throughout the shoot.

Around midnight, after a relaxing meal of seafood chowder, some of the cast and crew began to act oddly. Actor Bill
Paxton remembered that "people started laughing out loud,
others started crying, others were throwing up. Just as I started
to wonder what was happening, I started feeling weird myself.
Then I noticed Jim — one of his eyes was beet red like a
Terminator eye, and the other had no pupil at all."

Panic quickly set in with the suspicion that the shellfish in the chowder had been tainted. Sufferers were loaded into vans and taken to nearby Dartmouth General Hospital. Cameron himself had the presence of mind to induce vomiting quickly to purge whatever toxins he might have ingested. In total, eighty members of the *Titanic* cast and crew were treated at the hospital and released the next morning.

What was thought to be bad seafood turned out to be something much more sinister. The culprit was determined to be phencyclidine, better known as angel dust or PCP. When questioned about this by the media, Cameron quickly discounted the suggestions that there had been a deliberate attempt to sabotage his movie or target him personally.

For his part, Earle Scott, CEO of Quality Foods, the supplier of the chowder, believed that "it was that Hollywood crowd bringing all that psychedelic shit for their own amusement. I think it was a party that just got out of hand." Cast and crew had their own suspicions about a specific crew member who had been fired for dealing drugs on the set. However, Halifax police quickly declared the case closed.

When it came time to select a music composer for his epic film, Cameron turned to James Horner. Horner has scored seventy movies and TV shows (most recently *The Devil's Own* and *Ransom*) and won an Academy Award for his work on *Braveheart*. He worked with Cameron before on *Aliens*, and if he hadn't been particularly impressed with the *Titanic* screenplay, he probably wouldn't have worked with Cameron again. In 1987, when *Aliens* was being made, Cameron went to Horner with a demand that Horner thought was utterly ridiculous. "He [Cameron] told me that he needed over 100 minutes of music for his film, and he needed it in ten days," said Horner. "I told him that that was really pushing it, and that he probably shouldn't count on getting it that quickly. But Jim is … Jim, and if he says ten days, he means ten days. We fought constantly, though ultimately, the work was done, and I am quite proud of it. But I must say, I wasn't looking forward to the prospect of working with Jim Cameron again." However, upon reading the screenplay for *Titanic*, Horner was impressed and intrigued enough to call Cameron. The conversation began with apologies from both sides about the choppy working relationship the two had ten years previously, and they proceeded without further mention of it. Cameron had a few things to say to Horner in the way of guidance. His basic instructions to Horner were: no standard orchestration and absolutely no pop songs.

However, as the score proceeded, Horner felt that the movie needed something powerful at the end that would translate Rose's feelings into the proper cinematic perspective. He felt he needed a *song*.

To that end, he secretly commissioned a lyricist named Will Jennings to write a song that would encapsulate the main love theme of the film. Horner sang the resulting song for his friend, French-Canadian pop singer Céline Dion. Following his impromptu performance, Horner made an offer for her to record the song. All this was done without the sanction of James Cameron. The plan was to present the song to him already recorded, with the hope that Cameron would fall in love with it, and that it would be used in the film.

The song was recorded in May 1997 at a New York City recording studio, The Hit Factory. Céline Dion was unsettled by the secretive nature of this operation. Her nervousness was exacerbated by the fact that she had not been in a recording studio for quite awhile. Prior to performing "My Heart Will Go On" at the 1997 Grammy Awards, Dion stated, "I was shaking and sweating, and I couldn't control my voice. I was glad I felt those things because look what happened." The song turned out just the way Horner had hoped it would.

Sometime in June 1997, the song was played for Cameron. He was quite taken with it and immediately agreed to put it into the movie. However, Céline Dion and her manager/husband René Angelil were concerned that Dion was getting too exposed and too often identified as a sound-track specialist. A screening of *Titanic* was arranged for them. They were suitably blown away, and the song was added to the film and the sound-track album.

Even before Céline Dion became involved, Sony Classics bought the rights to the sound track. Horner had vigorously tried to persuade Polygram to buy the rights, given their success with the *Braveheart* sound track, but they passed. Nancy Zanini, VP, Polygram Classics, was asked about this decision and she responded, "In retrospect, it was the wrong decision, but at the time, nobody thought James Cameron could deliver a love story, and the price that they were asking for the rights (somewhere around $1 million) was just too steep for us." This was a decision that would cost them tens of millions of dollars in revenues.

The *Titanic* sound track is now the biggest-selling sound track in history. In fact, the album was Number One in at least fourteen countries, selling a staggering 15 million copies. It has outsold the entire Sony Classics catalog for the entire previous year, with no serious sign of a drop-off in sight.

When the word went out among the agents that James Cameron was going to make a huge romantic epic set aboard the *Titanic*, actors and actresses all over town were clamoring for a chance to look at the script. Twenty-two-year-old British actress Kate Winslet was one of them. Winslet was hardly a name that could be found on the Hollywood A-list of actresses, but ask any movie critic or journalist about her, and the response would be the same: Kate Winslet is a talented young actress who has already done remarkable work, while giving the impression that the best is still yet to come. She first gained widespread critical praise for her performance as the adolescent murderess in New Zealander Peter Jackson's brilliantly haunting 1994 film *Heavenly Creatures*. She has also done interesting work in Ang Lee's adaptation of *Sense and Sensibility* (1995) and in director Michael Winterbottom's little-seen but expertly executed adaptation of Thomas Hardy's *Jude the Obscure* in the 1996 film *Jude*. Winslet managed, through her agent, to get her hands on a copy of the script. By the time she finished reading it, she was in tears and on fire. She told herself that she absolutely had to be a part of this project. She called her agent and relayed that message. The agent, in turn, made some calls, but time was slipping away and Kate was getting impatient. She obtained a phone number for James Cameron so that she could make the pitch herself. She managed to reach Cameron in his car and launched into a speech about her need to do the movie. But Cameron cut her off, saying he was on his way to an appointment and couldn't talk. Winslet blurted out that he absolutely had to cast her, and that he was out of his mind if he didn't. This impressed Cameron enough to pull his car over so that he could discuss it with her further.

Winslet heard that Leonardo DiCaprio, who was closest to signing on to play Jack, was not entirely convinced this was something he wanted to do. Winslet tracked him down as well. Both happened to be at the Cannes Film Festival. She diligently sought his whereabouts and went to his hotel room to confront him. There, she told him that they had to do the movie together and that he was the only one to play Jack. Whether or not this incident of benign stalking had any effect on DiCaprio's decision is unknown. But the results of their on-screen pairing do speak for themselves.

During the arduous seven-month-long shoot in Mexico,

Winslet and DiCaprio became very close, as living in such close quarters and spending such an unnatural amount of time together is apt to do. Cameron was particularly impressed by the way the two young actors bonded together, helping each other through the difficult situation. "On a long shoot, especially when you hit month five, there is a siege mentality that takes over. They were really there for each other," he said.

Part of the movie's appeal is the interaction between the doomed lovers, Jack and Rose. It was aided enormously by the fact that Winslet and DiCaprio actually clicked immediately. Their friendship went way beyond romantic attraction. "We'd do the most ridiculous things to each other," said Winslet. "He'd be tickling me, groping me, winding me up. And I'd be doing the same thing back, grabbing his bum, making him laugh."

DiCaprio put it even more succinctly. "She was my best friend for seven months. We'd unload the stresses of the shoot to each other, vent to each other, and watch out for each other. Kate was just the perfect person to work with because she was one of the guys; it would have been much harder without her. We were partners."

The grueling shoot was not one big party for the actors — not by a long shot. During the scene where Jack tells Rose to close her eyes while poised high on the prow of the ship, Winslet was overcome by a severe attack of vertigo. She'd spent hours upon hours — an entire week — in a harness, suspended one hundred feet in the air. It was DiCaprio who calmed her down by repeating over and over again that they were safe.

Later on, during the scene where Rose valiantly retrieves a fire ax to release Jack from his handcuffs, Winslet remembered the difficulty, the sheer physical discomfort involved. "When I had to jump into that water with the ax, it was so cold that the reaction you see on screen was genuine. It was almost unbearable," she said.

There were scenes that required Winslet to swim through corridors — something that posed a different kind of hardship. As she was swimming, her feet would get tangled in her chiffon dress, and she would sink. Cameron quickly dealt with this, saying, "Fuck it, I'm not going to have one of my actresses drowning," and proceeded to attack the dress with a pair of scissors.

Despite the enormity of the project and the sheer physicality, for which she was unprepared, Winslet was quite forlorn when the experience ended. "It was April, and the movie had just wrapped. I was packing my stuff for the trip back to England. I just couldn't bring myself to believe that it was all over. I was never going to speak Rose's words again. It was a real feeling of loss that was quite profound," she said.

Still, there was some controversy surrounding Ms. Winslet. After wrapping the movie, she consented to an interview with the *Los Angeles Times*. She said, among other things, that she would never work for James Cameron ever again because of his bullying nature on the set. The piece only served to add fuel to the anti-*Titanic* sentiments that were piling up all over Hollywood. Winslet said later that the writer of the piece misinterpreted much of what she had said.

Cameron, whose demeanor allowed him to absorb bad things that were said or written about him without the need to fire back, shrugged this off philosophically. "Kate was just letting off steam. Every day, she would look out and see this small city, with these thousands of people all around, and she'd know that what it all boiled down to was what was going on in her eyes. She was under a lot of pressure."

As a result of his role in *Titanic*, her costar Leonardo DiCaprio, with his career already blossoming quite nicely, would be shot into a stratosphere orbited by only a scant few, — the Tom Hankses, the Tom Cruises, the Mel Gibsons. DiCaprio had done steadily impressive work since his big screen debut in the 1992 movie *This Boy's Life* in which he costarred with Robert DeNiro. In 1994, DiCaprio delivered a performance not a note short of brilliant in *What's Eating Gilbert Grape?*, playing a young handicapped boy in this poignant family drama that also starred Johnny Depp and Juliette Lewis. DiCaprio's performance was so convincing that some critics actually described him as "the young handicapped boy playing Depp's brother." What was enormously impressive about this young actor was the utter lack of vanity the performance required. It garnered DiCaprio his first Academy Award nomination for Best Supporting Actor. He went on to give towering performances in movies such as *The Basketball*

Diaries (1994), *Marvin's Room* (1996), *and Romeo + Juliet* (1996),
with a blip here and there in movies like *The Quick and the
Dead* (1995).

Romeo + Juliet had DiCaprio playing Shakespeare's Romeo
in a bizarre retelling of the story set in a semi-futuristic urban
sprawl called Verona Beach. His performance was fascinating
in that the Shakespearean dialogue rolled off his tongue like
it was his first language. The movie was a surprise hit, and
Leonardo DiCaprio suddenly had a rabid following of young
girls who wallpapered their bedrooms with his image.

It can be argued that DiCaprio is incapable of giving a
truly bad performance due to the innateness of his acting abil-
ities. However, his performance in *Titanic* was a considerable
distance from his best work. The reaction from fans when his
name was left off the list of Academy Award nominations for
Titanic might have been expected.

When asked about his *Titanic* experience, he was both
diplomatic and honest. He described the shoot as grunt work
and his "one and only occasion that I will ever be in such a
huge picture." He also mentioned being "grateful to be part
of such a wonderful movie that became bigger than all of us."
Just after the film wrapped, DiCaprio described, with wonder, a night on the set: "I was on the deck of this massive set,
and I was sitting on the railing looking out at this enormous
complex of buildings and sets that I was in the middle of. Then
this crane with a camera platform rose up, and there was Jim
Cameron sitting behind the camera calling out instructions.

And the platform just kept going up and up, and I sat there looking up and looking at everything, and I started asking myself what I had done in my life that had brought me to this place at this moment."

At his Malibu, California home, James Cameron has a highly sophisticated Avid-editing system. During the summer of 1997, it was put to constant use editing *Titanic*. For the first time in his career, Cameron was serving as his own editor in addition to writer, producer, and director. Taped to one of the editing machines was a razor blade — there for purposes of committing suicide — with a simple instruction next to it. "Use only if the film sucks."

Where did this journey begin? The spark was ignited in 1987 after Cameron watched the spectacular *National Geographic* documentary done by filmmaker Robert Ballard on the discovery of the wreck. "I remember the very first thing I saw of those images," said Cameron. "It was the robot that Robert Ballard used to go inside *Titanic*. And they showed a little bit of one of the chandeliers hanging there, and I thought, 'My God … that's incredible. They are using this space technology to go into the past like a time machine.' Something clicked right then." With a *Titanic* movie just floating around in his head, Cameron turned his underwater passion first to *The Abyss*. "While I was shooting *The Abyss*, I was meeting with Dr. Robert Ballard and discovering that there was a romance to the wreck that appealed to me. I started reading up on the

history, and that is very seductive. The event was almost perfectly novelistic. The elite of society was aboard, all the class
issues, the number of people that died in steerage. It had these
tensions and symbols. It was a goldmine." At the time, Cameron
jotted down an idea for a movie. "Do story with bookends of
present-day (wreckage) scene ... intercut with memory of a
survivor ... needs a mystery or a driving plot element."

The legend of the *Titanic* resurfaced in 1992 when Cameron
put *A Night to Remember* into his VCR. He started thinking
about his story set aboard the *Titanic* and quickly pounded
out a 167-page treatment. One of his chief objectives was to
do a movie that "signaled the end of the age of innocence, the
gilded Edwardian age, where science would allow us to master
the world." That summer, Cameron and his friend, renowned
underwater photographer Al Giddings, went to Russia to see
if they could persuade the Shirshov Institute to allow them
access to the deep-dive submersibles, the Mirs, for a trip to
the bottom of the Atlantic.

Jumping ahead to 1995 and the office of Peter Chernin,
chairman of Twentieth Century Fox, James Cameron was pitch-
ing his idea to Chernin and several other Fox creative executives. Cameron struggled to make his pitch as sexy as possible,
while keeping strictly to his vision. He maintained that (and
really believed it at the time) he could make this movie for
under $100 million. Chernin was intrigued, but he was ner-
vous about the size of the project. He would not give any kind
of go-ahead without further examination of the costs and risks

involved. Cameron then asked if he could have a few million dollars for development — not script development, but to fund a dive to the *Titanic* wreckage to get some actual footage of the ship. "It was an unusual request," said Cameron. "But not an unusual amount of money to get a major movie production going." The request was granted.

That September in the North Atlantic, just before noon on the eighth, the Mir 1, carrying James Cameron, Dr. Anatoly Sagalevitch, and a Russian engineer, plummeted to the ocean floor at a rate of ninety feet per minute. Two hours later, they crashed into a wall of iron. Getting their bearings, the submersible was maneuvered onto the deck of the wreckage. Upon Cameron's insistence, the submersible would settle on the deck of the *Titanic* daily while the team had their lunch.

Cameron and crew would spend twenty-five days on the North Atlantic and make twelve dives to the wreck to shoot footage, some of which ended up in the film. But as these first few dives progressed, Cameron started to connect with the wreck in a powerful way that took even him by surprise.

Excerpts of Cameron's personal diaries during the time of the dives were reprinted in *Wired*. Cameron wrote, "I just sat there, and I just started to cry, thinking about the dive and everything I'd seen. That's the moment that I let my technical guard down and I got kind of overwhelmed by it all.

"At that point, I realized that I was approaching it all wrong, and that the most important thing, maybe even more important than getting the footage, was capturing the emotional significance of the ship, what happened to it, and what happened to the people on it."

Being in such close proximity to the hulking wreckage was wondrous, but it was also very dangerous. The special camera housing developed by his brother Mike Cameron, head of Lightstorm Technologies, consisted of a solid titanium shell necessary for the camera to withstand 9 million pounds of pressure at that depth. Everyone was worried about this little device because there was no way you could test it. The Russian members of the crew nicknamed the camera rig "the cannon" because if the pressure were ever to cause the glass covering the lens to give way, the titanium housing would become a missile targeting whatever was directly in front of it. And because of what James Cameron was shooting, often that camera was pointed directly at their submersible. If that hunk of titanium had to hit their submersible, it would have meant a quick, gruesome death for all aboard.

This potential disaster almost came to pass during a dive on September 19. One of the two Mirs involved in the dive was getting a bit too close to the hull of the Titanic with the camera rig out front. The one thing that Mike Cameron had warned against was slamming the camera into the hull, but before they could swerve, there was a pronounced crunching sound as the camera crashed into the iron wall. James Cameron remembered, "I tensed for a moment waiting for the thunderclap of the implosion of the camera. It had been repeatedly pointed out to me that the implodable volume of the housing was so large that the shock wave from it could be enough to puncture the sub. We'd all be done in two ten-thousandths of a second."

James Cameron immediately aborted the dive and the second sub, the Mir 2, was maneuvered directly to the surface. When Cameron and his team in the Mir 1 tried to begin their ascent, nothing happened. It seemed their batteries had drained during a move through heavy currents. They were dangerously low on power and in a complete stall 12,640 feet below sea level. Everything using valuable power had to be shut down immediately, and they sat in the dark at the bottom of the Atlantic for half an hour. Finally, the Russian pilot rigged up a system that used the emergency ballast to propel them toward the surface, but that gave them only fifty feet per second of rise. It took them well over four hours to get to the surface.

By this point, everyone involved was getting weary and starting to question their continued presence at the wreck. Production designer John Bruno summed it up best in his notes from September 25. "Here we are, a bunch of Hollywood assholes, driving around the *Titanic* like she's a theme-park attraction, bumping into things and generally ogling at the scope and scale of this disaster, creating our own reality of the events. We're voyeurs, staring at the hulk of this great ship as though she was a creature in a zoo. The Mirs have made this all as easy as a drive in the park. But we must remember that the *Titanic* is a dangerous wreck in a dangerous location. I think she is growing weary of our antics."

Despite this, they shot some of the best footage ever taken of the sunken liner. Upon viewing the footage, Cameron was absolutely delighted. He went back to Fox, continuing his feverish pitch to get his dream movie under way.

Since Cameron was already decided on the cost-effective plan of actually building a near full-scale model of the ship, the only thing remaining was a place to build it. The site would have to be vast and preferably near or on water. Cameron looked at various blimp hangars and large rock quarries. He even visited plants used to construct submarines in Poland, Australia, and England.

What was finally settled on was the construction of a full state-of-the-art production facility in Rosarito Beach, Mexico. The size of this studio was staggering, covering forty acres with three complete soundstages, a 32,000-foot wet stage with a 5-million-gallon tank, and a full set of production offices including dressing rooms and storage buildings. Beside these structures was to be a massive 17-million-gallon outdoor water tank — the biggest in the world by a long shot. The studio cost an estimated $40 million.

Fox liked the idea of coming out of this project with a studio as an ongoing asset. But they still weren't sold on the project. The costs seemed to be creeping up past the $100-million mark. Cameron came back with suggestions and offers of where he could trim the project to keep costs in check. Fox countered the offer by suggesting that Cameron try to get some stars connected to the project. Cameron was looking for an "Audrey Hepburn type" for the role of Rose and a "Jimmy Stewart type" for Jack. Before connecting with Kate Winslet, Cameron considered actresses such as Gwyneth Paltrow, Gabrielle Anwar, and Claire Danes. The actors being considered for Jack were Matthew McConaughey and *Batman*'s Robin, Chris O'Donnell. But Cameron felt both these actors were too old for what he had in mind.

Casting agent Mali Finn suggested Leonardo DiCaprio to Cameron. Cameron met with DiCaprio, but it didn't go well initially. Cameron had DiCaprio and Winslet get together for a reading, but Leo refused to read with her. Cameron was persistent, and DiCaprio finally read through the scene once but then let his attention wander and remained unfocused for the rest of the session. "But for one split second," says Cameron, "a shaft of light came down from the heavens and lit up the forest."

DiCaprio resisted the role, the movie, and the director for quite awhile. He thought the character of Jack was uninteresting and soft. He suggested to Cameron that the character be given a limp and a mysterious, darker past. Cameron shot back, "No, I will not give him a tic or a limp or all the other things you are suggesting. The character has to be as uncomplicated as possible." Leo was finally persuaded to do the movie. The fact that he was to be paid his first million-dollar up-front salary probably figured in the decision, but reports from the set attested to the fact that DiCaprio constantly questioned Cameron's direction. If Cameron described a scene in which Kate Winslet jumped from the lifeboat back onto the deck of the sinking *Titanic* by saying, "You don't know she's going to jump until she jumps," Leo would shoot back, "But I can see it in her face. I would see it coming."

He got the job done, and he delivered the performance that was expected of him. But Cameron was frustrated by his young star's demeanor. "Every time we're about to do water work, Leo gets sick," was something Cameron was heard to say. He was also heard commenting sarcastically on the fact that there must have been a shipment of important new video games to explain DiCaprio's chronic lateness to the set.

The rest of the cast was an interesting mix of character actors and Hollywood types. Bill Paxton, a James Cameron regular, took the small role of Brock Lovett to work with his friend again. But he was also fascinated by the legend of the great ship.

Somewhat forgotten Hollywood actress Gloria Stuart was chosen to play the 101-year-old Rose Calvert. What was ironic was the fact that the eighty-seven-year-old Stuart was forced to endure over two hours per day being made up to look older, even though she could have easily passed for the old Rose without any makeup at all. James Cameron had interviewed many women for this role, but he was impressed by the mischievous attitude Stuart brought to it. Stuart had worked with directors like John Ford, Busby Berkeley, and James Whale as well as with actors such as James Cagney and Boris Karloff. When asked about *Titanic*, she smiled and described it as "the icing on the cake." Stuart was nominated for an Oscar for her work, making her part of Oscar trivia history. Since Kate Winslet was also nominated, it was the first time ever that two actors have been nominated in the same year for playing the same character in the same movie.

For the real-life characters, Cameron chose three solid performers: veteran British actor Bernard Hill as Captain E.J. Smith; Canadian-born actor Victor Garber as Thomas Andrews; and Jonathan Hyde as J. Bruce Ismay. Bernard Hill, seen in such films as *The Bounty, Ghandi*, and most recently, the underrated *The Ghost and the Darkness*, bore a physical resemblance to the real Captain E.J. Smith. The real Smith had a seafaring career that spanned forty years. He had never been in an accident, had never been reprimanded, had never even seen a ship founder — until April 15, 1912. Garber injected a remarkable poignancy into his role as the master shipbuilder of the *R.M.S. Titanic*, especially in the scenes just after the collision with the iceberg. Jonathan Hyde captured just the right amount of upper-class arrogance as the White Star Lines manager who managed to selfishly steal away into a lifeboat and survive the sinking. Ismay was famous for uttering the historic line "The maiden voyage of the *Titanic* must make headlines."

Cameron's creative team on *Titanic* was, for the most part, made up of people he had worked with before. Originally, ace cinematographer Caleb Deschanel was hired to photograph *Titanic*, but he left the production after the Halifax leg of the shoot because his style of working clashed severely with Cameron's. Russell Carpenter, who had shot *True Lies* and the live-action *T2-3-D* scenes for Cameron, replaced him. Cameron went to special-effects coordinator Thomas Fisher because they worked successfully together on the similarly complex *Terminator 2: Judgment Day*. Production designer Peter Lamont received an Oscar nomination for his work on Cameron's *Aliens* and worked with him again on *True Lies*. He was absolutely delighted to work on *Titanic* because "this was a designers' dream, such a rich, lush palate and such a powerful, committed, passionate director. This is the kind of movie you want to do, hopefully, once in your career."

One important member of his crew with whom he had not worked before was costume designer Deborah Scott. Scott threw herself into the challenge of re-creating this era, but it was not without moments of pause. "We filled the whole office with pictures of actual passengers on the *Titanic*, and we would study them very analytically. I suddenly thought, 'We're not looking at research here. We're looking at the real people who were on the ship, who lived in those exact moments.' It was eerie. It became more than just making a movie — you wanted to live up to history."

In May 1996, Cameron finally got the official go-ahead to begin work on *Titanic*. Since he had a reputation for spending more than his budget allotted, and since the number guys at Fox were already forecasting an expenditure much greater than was officially being stated, they wanted to seek out a partner to help share the risk. They went first to Universal Pictures, and while Universal chairman Casey Silver was very impressed by Cameron's wonderfully readable screenplay, he was worried by the way the proposed arrangement was structured. The deal tabled allowed Fox to retain complete control over the project. This didn't sit well with Universal, and it ultimately caused them to shy away from the deal. In retrospect, it will probably cost Universal about half a billion dollars, but at the time, it was the right decision.

Meanwhile, Sherry Lansing and John Goldwyn at Paramount heard that the *Titanic* project was in need of a partner. They quickly stepped in, willing to come on board in exchange for the domestic distribution rights. Just as the deal was about to be signed, Viacom Entertainment Group (owner of Paramount Pictures) chairman Jonathan Dolgen threw in one last codicil. He insisted that Paramount be on the hook for no more than $65 million. Anything over that would have to be covered by Fox. Fox quickly agreed because they wanted a partner, even if the terms weren't exactly equitable.

In November 1996, at the massive Rosarito Beach studios, Cameron was about to commence filming a gigantic scene. The replica of *Titanic* was raised high in the air, sending about a hundred stunt people careening all over the deck, bouncing off cushioned railings and fixtures. It was on this evening that recently appointed Fox chairman and CEO Bill Mechanic decided to pay a visit to the set to impose some budget restrictions, a move Mechanic deemed necessary because it looked like the production of the movie could spin wildly out of control.

Cameron was not pleased to have studio people in his midst, but he met with Mechanic during a break in shooting to talk business. Mechanic presented Cameron with a detailed memo that suggested several cost-saving cuts. "If you want to cut the film, you will have to fire me. And to fire me, you'll have to kill me," was Cameron's response to the memo. Cameron reportedly started smashing things until the executive left. Mechanic headed back to Los Angeles that night.

A few days later, Cameron called Mechanic suggesting a few cuts of his own that would help save money. One strange, but ultimately telling, piece of give-and-take involved the scene in the script that had Jack teaching the prim and proper Rose how to spit like a man. The studio wasn't crazy about the scene, thinking it was unnecessarily vulgar and out of place — a scene that could be easily cut. Cameron was adamant about retaining the scene because he felt it was a wonderful moment in their relationship. He was so set on keeping the scene in the shooting schedule that he allegedly gave up building another huge section of his Titanic mock-up as a concession to save his beloved spitting scene.

On the set in Mexico, Cameron allowed himself the luxury of being a man obsessed. It was almost as if he knew this was *the* film. *Titanic* would make him the filmmaker who didn't need cyborgs, aliens, or Arnold Schwarzenegger to make a meaningful, successful film. He was constantly grabbing a hand-held camera and personally filming shots — something he could get away with in union-isolated Mexico. James Cameron has always been a hands-on director, but this was different. This was deep passion being played out. For example, the sketches drawn by Jack Dawson in the movie were actually done by Cameron. In fact, it was Cameron's hand doing the drawing in the scene where Jack sketches a reclining nude of Rose.

By March 22, 1997 Cameron was setting up the last massive shot of the movie. The scene involved an underwater explosion that caused tons of water to come crashing through a tempered-glass skylight. For this sequence, Cameron donned his wet suit and shot the footage himself with a hand-held camera on his shoulder. This sequence was cause for some rumbling. Prior to the take, the stunt coordinator's assessment of the situation described hazards that included the risk of drowning. This dangerously complex scene was being set up by exhausted crew members who had been working fifteen days without a break. It was reported that several crew members fell asleep during the morning meeting detailing the dangers of the upcoming sequence. However, *Titanic* producer Jon Landau dismissed these concerns, saying long working hours on movie shoots are entirely commonplace.

Even though Cameron was caught up in the razzle-dazzle and technology of creating the film, cast and crew members were noticing that this was a different James Cameron than they had known from previous experience or by reputation. Jim Muro, a Steadicam operator who had worked with

Cameron three times before, observed the director at work with his actors in the scene where the characters played by Kate Winslet, Billy Zane, Frances Fisher, and David Warner first arrive on the ship. "Jim has made an incredible leap forward in terms of sensitivity to subject matter."

Actor Billy Zane, who plays the evil Cal Hockley, was equally impressed and surprised by the director he was working with as opposed to the director he had anticipated working with. "It really wasn't what I was expecting, to have this guy be such an actor's director." Zane was constantly amazed; he had never worked with anyone like Cameron. "It was a sink-or-swim energy on the set, so to speak, said Zane. "Jim's the coach you want to please, who will kick your ass on the field but will be the first one to celebrate the touchdown." Zane, awed by the thoroughness of his director, marveled, "He's a very clever man. He'd be setting up seventeen cameras, barking commands at five hundred actors and extras, and suddenly he stops, puts on the brakes, and applies, by hand, a perfect trickle of blood down an extra's face."

Cameron's vision in re-creating this event was so singular that each scene took on an air of historical importance. While directing a scene in the water, where the boat had gone under and the survivors in the lifeboats were struggling with what should be done next, Cameron yelled into his microphone, "Okay, I want you guys to talk it up, and I want the oars to hit the people in the boat so they have to get up and move." He called for the cameras to roll. "The oars should be uneven.

C'mon, you guys are too good! It's an emergency evacuation!
You've never done this before, you're flailing, you're scared!"
Finally, he called "cut!" and reset the scene. He turned and
remarked to someone that this was the part of the *Titanic* story
that no one had seen. He believed that when the ship went
down and a thousand people went into the water, those survivors in the lifeboats tried to get away as fast as they could,
not because they were concerned about being sucked down
with the ship (they couldn't have known that would happen),
but because they simply wanted to get away. Cameron believed
that the lifeboats tried to get as far away from the screaming
masses in the water as fast as they could. When they were
ready for take two, Cameron yelled into the microphone,
"Okay, I want you all to flail 10 percent more than last time."

One of the fascinating things *Titanic* evoked in its viewers was the question of what each of us would have done had
we been on the deck of the great ship that night. It was a
question James Cameron had asked himself many times. It
was his belief that if this tragedy happened today, men taking
their places in the lifeboats would trample the women uncer-
emoniously . He believed the women-and-children-first valor
that was evident the night of April 15, 1912 in the crew and
gentlemen on deck was admirable yet gone forever. As for his
personal reaction, "I don't think I would have tried to take
anyone's place. But once I saw that there were boats being
launched half full (the first lifeboat launched had a capacity
of sixty-five, yet was lowered with only twenty-eight people

aboard), I think I would have dove into the water and swam to the nearest boat with extra room. There were only four people who actually did that. I'd like to think that I am smart enough and together enough to have done that."

From a production standpoint, if Cameron was pressured to compromise on one area of detail, the studio could then counter the need for strident accuracy if certain things could be faked successfully. From that point of view, it certainly was in Cameron's interest to be a steadfast as possible in insisting on accurate detail. But from a dramatic standpoint, he took some liberties that were perhaps necessary in the construction of a dramatic piece, but were not so palatable to the surviving relatives of those involved in Cameron's dramatic-tinkering scenes. Take the case of Scott Murdoch, nephew of *Titanic's* First Officer William McMaster Murdoch. Now in his eighties and still living in the small town of Dalbeattie in Scotland where his uncle came from, he was quite horrified by the way Cameron had portrayed his family member. First Officer Murdoch was historically remembered for having been a hero, helping women and children to safety before going down with the ship. In Cameron's script, First Officer Murdoch accidentally shoots a third-class passenger in a crush of panic. He then salutes his ship, puts a pistol to his head, pulls the trigger, and then tumbles lifelessly into the water. A stone monument recalled the courage of one of their native sons in the face of unspeakable tragedy. Family members wondered why Cameron didn't fictionalize the character altogether or why the scene didn't use another entirely fictitious character. The National Maritime Museum in London backed the story of the Murdoch family and remarked, "It is a shame that Cameron felt it necessary to rewrite the story in the name of good drama."

This situation was resolved, sort of, when Twentieth Century Fox executive Scott Neeson issued a letter to the people of Dalbeattie stating, "Officer Murdoch was a decent, responsible, and very human hero and should remain a source of pride for Dalbeattie and in the memories of all those who knew of his life." Also in the envelope was a check for $8,000.

Once the shooting was finished, Cameron headed to his editing machine for twelve days of cutting. He had so much footage that he completely used up the memory capacity of three of his Avid-editing rigs. He worked in seventeen-hour shifts, cutting down the footage and self-administering high-octane vitamin shots to keep his energy up. While Cameron worked at this, eighteen of the best visual-effects shops in the movie business were busy with the over five hundred special-effects shots that Cameron had ordered.

Mike Kanfer, one of the guys in charge of those effects at Digital Domain, remembered this challenge: "We thought *Apollo 13* was hard. But we could do that stuff in a weekend compared to what we were doing with *Titanic*." Kanfer's title was Digital Compositing Supervisor, and he described the first year on the project as "one long deadline." The decision to delay the release of the film was a great relief to him and his team. "We really got the chance to make sure this stuff got done right," said Kanfer. Some of these special-effects shots lasted thirty seconds or more. "That was quite unusual. In the old days, we wouldn't dare hold an effects shot any longer than three or four seconds." But the biggest challenge of the entire project as far as Kanfer was concerned was the interaction of computer-generated people with real actors. Also tremendously challenging was making the hull of the ship interact with the water, again using computer-generated images.

As the pressure of releasing the most expensive movie in history mounted, the strain started to show on the overworked, overburdened army of computer-effects technicians. Mistakes started to surface. In one incident, expensive computer-generated footage had to be completely redone once it was discovered that it portrayed the *Titanic* sailing in the wrong direction — toward Southampton rather than away from the city. In another episode, Cameron hit the roof when shown a shot of the ship sinking with one of the propellers slowly rotating. He angrily told his crew that anyone who knew *anything* about the *Titanic* knew that the propellers were still by that time. The shot was redone.

With all the money that had been spent and no end in sight, the heat in the executive offices at Fox and Paramount was starting to rise. As the July 2 release date drew nearer, the temperature reached the boiling point. It became clear that more editors and facilities were needed, and the two studios fought over who would pay for these extras.

When it was announced that the movie would not be

ready for the original release date, Fox argued for an August release. They wanted the returns to start coming in as quickly as possible. Paramount argued that by August, the lucrative summer-moviegoing season was almost over. Paramount suggested a November release. Fox shot back that this simply would not work for them since they already had their two highest profile movies for the year slated for November release (*Alien Resurrection* and *Anastasia*). During the 1997 Cannes Film Festival, it was reported that the discussion about the release of *Titanic* between Bill Mechanic of Fox and Rob Friedman, head of marketing and distribution for Paramount, became so heated that it looked as if a fistfight might commence at any moment. It was finally decided during this "discussion" that the new release date would be December 19. Right off the bat, the delay added almost $4 million to the budget in interest charges alone. But the delay also had a ripple effect throughout Hollywood. The summer months were the most lucrative for the studios, and all their big-budget crowd grabbers were released during these months. Each weekend was plotted. For example, if Universal was releasing *Lost World* on a particular weekend, then the other studios held back their big films until the dust settled. When *Titanic* was scheduled to open on July 2, to capitalize on the July 4 holiday weekend, no other studio was interested in putting anything out against it. When *Titanic* was delayed, it left a gaping hole in the holiday release schedule which caused the other studios to start moving their movies around the calendar like chess pieces.

Oscar considerations were definitely a factor, and Paramount started gearing up for a December publicity blitz that is said to have cost upward of $60 million. Then they were trumped once again by Fox. It was announced in September that Twentieth Century Fox would one up Paramount by officially premiering *Titanic* at the upcoming Tokyo Film Festival on November 1, almost two months before the much-anticipated North American debut of the movie. Paramount was angry. They knew that every major critic in the world would be heading for Tokyo to see the movie. What if the critical response was negative? What if the audiences didn't like it? That would leave Paramount with the tough chore of marketing the North American release amid bad press and bad word of mouth. All involved waited for the Tokyo Film Festival and the reports on how *Titanic* was received.

It would turn out to be a stroke of genius on the part of Twentieth Century Fox. Both James Cameron and Leonardo DiCaprio were scheduled to make an appearance, and crowds of adoring Leonardo DiCaprio fans, fans who'd recently fallen in love with him because of his performance in *Romeo + Juliet*, lined the streets waiting for the object of their affection.

As the lights went down and the film began. Cameron was anxious and nervous, but confident in his work. After the screening, he quickly gathered up the last three reels of the film for shipment back to LA where the sound and color would be tinkered with one more time.

Of the festival crowd, many loved *Titanic*, others thought

the love story was weak, but all were blown away by the awesome visual effects. The early reviews were positive. Todd McCarthy of *Variety* wrote that *Titanic* was a triumph of cinematic technology finally being used on a film that was character-driven rather than effects-driven. He praised Cameron for having the guts to even attempt something on such a grand scale. However, the early reviews were not what Fox and Paramount had anticipated. All involved hoped this movie would be called great; what was being said was that it was pretty good.

As usual on a Cameron film shoot, the crew would have shirts made making light of the legend of James Cameron. Some of the sayings printed on the shirts included: "It's a timing thing. I don't care if it has any organic emotional reality or not," and "No animals were hurt during the making of this film, but the actors were tossed around like Styrofoam cups." But the best of the bunch had to be "Jim's a hands-on director … and I have the bruises to prove it."

On the massive Mexican set, it was clear that Cameron was not only making a movie; he was realizing a dream. Despite his iron will, there were times when he worried. "There's a chance that the movie with either be all things to everybody or nothing to anybody," he was heard saying during a break in shooting on the *Titanic* replica. "Not enough action for the action crowd, not enough romance for the romance crowd." Yet another time, while sitting on a huge crane, he remarked,

"I hope we make people feel like they've had a good time. Not a good time in the sense that they've seen a *Batman* movie, but a good time in the sense that they've had their emotions kind of checked and the plumbing still works." This perhaps expressed his true feelings.

The Mexican set was a sight that could only be described as surreal — like a mirage. The model of the *Titanic*, built to nine-tenths scale, seemingly perched on the beach against the relief of the sea, was built at the end of miles upon miles of desolate sand. Actually, the model was held in a 17-million-gallon water tank at the ocean's edge, providing a 270-degree view of the "sea" around the ship. Since this huge model was detailed down to the rivets on the starboard side only, scenes involving the port side had to be shot carefully. The port-side scenes were also shot on the starboard side, which meant that everything had to be reversed — all the lettering on signs, all the lettering on uniforms, everything. In order to simulate the sinking of the *Titanic*, the front half of the replica that was built on the beach was separated from the rest of the ship in such a way that it could be lowered into a forty-foot hole on a hydraulic system.

Fox Studios Baja, as the studio was finally called, was dubbed 'The one-hundred-day studio' because it took only that long to erect. When *Titanic* left the studio, the James Bond film *Tomorrow Never Dies* moved in for some shooting. Ironically, both films opened on December 19 and battled it out for the Christmas season movie dollar.

Even though this 770-foot re-creation of part of the great ship gets most of the attention, there were several other models that were constructed for the film. While the monster model was being constructed in Mexico, Digital Domain was building a one-twentieth scale, forty-foot-long model of the pristine ship. There was another one-twentieth-scale model constructed to represent the wreckage at the bottom of the Atlantic. That model was suspended upside down in a studio to make it easier to work with for the motion control camera operators. The results were spectacular in that you could not tell which footage was actually shot on the bottom of the Atlantic, or which was the result of motion-control cameras in the studio. All the models were extraordinarily detailed, having been constructed from the original plans for the original ship.

As impressive as the enormity of the craftsmanship involved in creating the models was, what was truly mind-boggling was the attention to detail Cameron applied to the endeavor. During the shooting of the voyage scenes, etiquette experts were constantly on the set to coach the actors playing the guests (how to walk as they would have walked, how to hold champagne flutes, etc.) and the actors playing the service staff. Everything from the furniture to the flatware was exact. In fact, the companies who manufactured these items for White Star Lines provided Cameron with the re-creations. The sale of all these props used by Cameron was another by-product of the staggering success of the film. A catalog was printed, and interested consumers could buy everything from coat hangers to life jackets or even sections of the massive replica of *Titanic*.

A constant irritation to Cameron during the Mexican leg of the shoot were the reports coming from the set concerning rampant injuries and foolhardy disregard for the safety of his cast and crew. "The thing that bothered me most were the reports of widespread accidents and injuries and even deaths — lack of safety and reckless disregard for human life and all that sort of thing. What I found ironic about that was, I've always had a reputation as one of the safest directors in Hollywood." Despite that reputation, reports from disgruntled crew members, actors, and extras started filtering home from the Mexican set. Matters were made even worse when San Diego television station KGTV reported that ten people working on the movie were injured badly enough to require surgery. Officials from Twentieth Century Fox described the reports as "absolutely untrue."

Jeffrey Godsick, senior vice president of publicity at Fox, was quoted in the *Hollywood Reporter* as saying that there had been "eight or nine" accidents during the construction of the studio facility, not actually during the production of the movie. He went on to say that for a project the size of *Titanic*, there had been remarkably few accidents and that none of cast members had been injured.

The Screen Actors Guild (SAG) took a less sanguine view and was concerned enough about the rumors to set in motion their own investigation. The concern grew when SAG representatives, upon arrival in Mexico, were told about extras that had been asked to perform stunts such as jumping off tilted decks into the water a few stories below. This would have been a flagrant breach of the Guild's contract had the movie been made in the United States. SAG had no jurisdiction in Mexico, so it was unusual for the union to send people there for the express purpose of investigating the working conditions on the *Titanic* set and to bring to bear "every possible pressure on Twentieth Century Fox, Mexico, the Mexican performers' union, and the International Federation of Actors to substantially and immediately improve these conditions."

Much was made of the SAG's investigation of James Cameron and the *Titanic* set and about the fact that SAG had no real jurisdiction in Mexico in the first place. But little was reported as to the outcome of the investigation. "We conclude that director/producer James Cameron has taken extraordinary measures to ensure the health and safety of the cast and crew" was the statement issued by the SAG just before they packed up and left Mexico for Hollywood.

During the shoot, Cameron tried to respond to these charges by writing a personal letter that appeared in the *Los Angeles Times*. Addressing the film community and the media, the letter stated, "It seems to have become a dirty concept these days to work too hard, to care too much, to give your all." He went on to defend directly the safety issue by curtly writing, "Am I driven? Yes, absolutely. Out of control? Never. Unsafe? Not on my watch."

Hot on the heels of the health and safety issue was the debate on just how much James Cameron's *Titanic* actually cost. Was it $200 million? Was it $285 million? Was it actually over $300 million? Cameron was asked this question in a suite in London's Dorchester Hotel the day after the spectacularly successful Royal premiere of *Titanic*. (Prince Charles described the movie as one of the finest he's ever seen.) "People are seeing $285 million — I don't even know where that comes from. It's pure speculation. I checked before I flew in here and the final budget was $200 million. I was kind of hoping that we were somewhat under the $200 mark, but we're hovering on the cusp," said Cameron.

On Sunday afternoon, November 23, 1997, a special Toronto screening of *Titanic* was scheduled to start at 3 p.m. Many members of the press were in attendance because James Cameron was rolling into Toronto for the next couple of days to do as many interviews as he possibly could. There was a tangible excitement in the air; this movie that everyone had read, heard, and talked about for a year was about to flash across the screen.

From the opening images, the audience knew they were indeed sitting through the movie event of the year. But by the end of the 197-minute film, they knew they had witnessed the film event perhaps of the decade or beyond. Viewers were divided on whether *Titanic* was a great movie or simply a good movie. The final hour was filled with terror, majesty, and jaw-dropping visual virtuosity, but the love story felt juvenile and contrived. Leonardo DiCaprio and Kate Winslet were fun to watch as Jack and Rose, but the performances of Billy Zane and Bill Paxton seemed part of a different movie. Eighty-seven-year-old Hollywood veteran Gloria Stuart hit just the right notes in her role. But what really stood out were the haunting images Cameron showed us. Some of his scenes literally took our breath away.

The next day, in a suite in the Four Seasons Hotel in Toronto, James Cameron was hustled back and forth from one room to another to speak with one TV interviewer after another. Cameron took the questions — some ridiculous, others serious — in stride, providing thoughtful answers. When asked about the juvenile nature of the love story, Cameron bristled and gave a measured answer about teenage romances and how they could function on two or three levels of interpretation. If "juvenile" meant "pure," that was exactly what he was going for. One interviewer began her chat by saying, "I can imagine the enormous difficulties you encountered making this movie." Cameron shot her a straight, steely look and replied, "No, you can't."

Cameron left Toronto and headed to Chicago for the next leg of the publicity tour. This press tour, which started in Tokyo on November 1, resumed on the weekend of November 15 and 16 in New York City, with stops in England and Russia and all points in between. Looking back, General Cameron waged a brilliant campaign.

What everyone sat and waited for now was the December 19 release. Fox and Paramount were cautiously optimistic, but MGM/UA was downright nervous. For them, *Titanic* represented competition of potentially staggering proportions. MGM/UA had gone from the greatest of Hollywood glory to the kind of desperate clawing that usually signals the death knell of a studio. But they managed to stay afloat, prospering in fits and starts. The starts came in the form of the lucrative James Bond series. With Pierce Brosnan now firmly established as the best Bond since Sean Connery (Brosnan's first outing as 007 was the most successful in the history of the franchise), these movies were the feather in the fairly bald MGM/UA crown. The latest Bond movie, *Tomorrow Never Dies*, was also set for release on December 19. It was naturally assumed that because Bond had such a worldwide following (made even more attractive by the inclusion of British bad guy Jonathan Pryce and Asian action queen Michelle Yeoh), and because of *Titanic's* bloated running time, Bond would financially top Cameron's movie.

December 19, the day of the release showdown, arrived. Studio bosses watched the figures and the lineups. MGM Canada boss Julia Perry and her publicity coordinator Mary Marentic started checking the theater records directly following the first screening. For MGM, the news from Toronto theaters was good: Bond was making more money locally. Then, on the following Monday morning, the mind-boggling figures started rolling in. Weekend one: *Titanic* brought in $29 million compared to $23 million for *Tomorrow Never Dies*. The floodgates opened and the *Titanic* juggernaut rumbled through. By the second weekend, *Titanic*'s earnings reached $88 million, averaging $34 million per week. By week eleven, the total earnings topped $402 million.

At well over $600 million in domestic box office returns, as of June, 1998, *Titanic* was the all-time earnings champ. *Jurassic Park* was left behind after $357.1 million. (It took *Jurassic Park* sixty-seven days to reach the $300-million mark. *Titanic* hauled that figure in just forty-four days). *Titanic* had also beaten *Jurassic Park*'s overseas take of $500 million.

Prior to the release of *Titanic*, when asked about the financial chance this movie stood, Fox executive Bill Mechanic, the guy taking the most studio heat, replied, "We're wishful that this movie can make a small profit. It is a terrific movie, so it certainly has the chance to break even." After the movie crossed the $700-million worldwide tally, Mechanic was quoted as saying, "Who knows how far it will go? I'm just grateful for where it is. I took enough shit for an entire year. I never wavered. I always knew we had a great movie."

But what of the critical response to the film? From the outset, this seemed to be one of those films that would be received with either wide-open arms and rave reviews or a lukewarm reception. It seemed unlikely that anyone would outright hate it. Interestingly, the early critical response was somewhat over-the-top praise from respected critics not usually given to such gushing. Janet Maslin of *The New York Times* wrote, "*Titanic* is the first spectacle in decades that honestly invites comparison to *Gone With the Wind*. What a rarity that makes it in today's world of meaningless gimmicks and short attention spans: a huge, thrilling three-and-a-quarter-hour experience that unerringly lures viewers into the beauty and heartbreak of its lost world." David Ansen of *Newsweek* raved, "The allure of *Titanic* is its invitation to swoon at a scale of epic moviemaking that is all but obsolete." David Kehr of *The New York Daily News* said, "*Titanic* is magnificent. An overwhelming visual, aural, and emotional experience."

Even dissenting opinions usually ended on a high note. British critic Rupert Howe wrote in the excellent British film magazine *Neon*, "*Titanic* may not be as clever as Cameron thinks it is, but — since they stopped making this kind of film about thirty years ago — there's nothing out there any bigger." A strong anti-*Titanic* sentiment was expressed in *Film Comment* magazine by Kent Jones: "Actually, many people whose opinions I respect think very highly of *Titanic*, but I marvel at their eagerness to see past its dramatic crudity, its profoundly rotten dialogue, and its rough patches of Saturday morning animation in order to knit together a popular masterpiece. I have the impression that everyone feels as if they are *obliged* to like it."

But this movie has proven itself to be critic-proof, as it were, and the cash just rolled in by the bushel. Cameron, upon growing used to the records his movie was breaking, started looking at the response to *Titanic* with a philosophical bent. "Some people are mistaking *Titanic*'s success for the return of the spectacle. But it's more than that. This movie messes you up emotionally — and audiences like to get their emotions messed up at the movies."

Where will all this cash go? How will it be split up among the two studios that backed *Titanic*? Even though Twentieth Century Fox spent a great deal more on the movie than their partners at Paramount (estimates put Fox kicking in around $215 million and Paramount around $115 million — $65 million toward the budget and another $50 million in domestic marketing) the earnings will be split fifty-fifty until Paramount gets its $115-million investment back. After that, monies from all related sources will go into a giant pot that will be split sixty-forty in favor of Twentieth Century Fox, the larger of the risk takers. It appears that both studios will easily clear in excess of a $100 million profit.

Titanic kept its Number One position for a record-shattering eleven straight weekends with a $200 million take in North America alone. By this time, the movie had opened throughout the world, and the global take was nearing the $900-million mark. It was clear that *Titanic* would blast away every existing box-office record the world over by becoming the first movie to take in excess of $1 billion. And what made the statistics even more staggering was the speed with which this happened.

How could this be explained? The movie was good, but not *that* good. It defied explanation. This was a movie that was well over three hours long, yet teenagers were going to see *Titanic* three, four, five times or more. As James Cameron acknowledged, this movie had crossed over into that magical place known as cultural phenomenon. "I'm certainly mystified by what has happened. But I'm enjoying the ride. Realistically, I'll probably never experience this kind of thing again," said Cameron. Feminist spokesperson Camille Paglia described her views on the phenomenon: "People are sick and tired of shallow, postmodernist irony and cynicism; people are ready for big passions, grand opera, big sweeping statements." Renowned critic Pauline Kael simply stated, "It's square in a way that people seem to have been longing for."

On March 7, 1998 James Cameron was granted the title of Best Director at the Director's Guild Awards in Los Angeles. A pleased, obviously thoughtful Cameron took the dais and made a speech tending toward subtle self-congratulation: "I used to always say that I made movies and not films. *Remains of the Day* is a film; *Terminator 2: Judgment Day* is a movie. Now that I have this, I have to admit that I may have inadvertently made a film." It was predicted earlier in the year that director Curtis Hanson would win for *LA Confidential*, but the tide had turned, so to speak.

Cameron was asked about the money end of the *Titanic* juggernaut as he strolled into the Shrine Auditorium for the Academy Awards ceremony, and he replied, "I think there will be something coming my way, not nearly as much as there would have been if I didn't give back the points, but that was all worth it in that I was allowed to continue to make the movie that I had to make."

And what about all the fuss that was made about James Cameron giving back his salary plus his profit participation. Well, that too was corrected as the movie smashed record after record. Actually, when Cameron gave back his salary and profit participation points, it was after Fox executives concluded that at the rate Cameron was spending, *Titanic* would never make a dime. Cameron decided to affect the giveback as a show of good faith, but the contract stipulated that if the movie were to gross over $500 million, then his director's fee would be reinstated — along with his points. It was a win-win situation for the studio. The sum that Cameron would receive for making the biggest movie in history was then estimated about $50 million, but that figure was later revised to upward of $100 million. But the morning after the Oscars, James Cameron had yet to see any of that money.

Leonardo DiCaprio and Kate Winslet would also receive, reportedly, bonuses in excess of $1 million for inspiring the romantic fantasies of a teenage global audience. DiCaprio's asking price had soared to the $20-million range since *Titanic* set sail.

What was left to see was how the Hollywood community, namely the Academy of Motion Picture Arts and Sciences, would view the movie. *Titanic* was nominated for nine Golden Globe Awards (a Hollywood Foreign Press Association awards show) and it won, surprisingly, four awards including awards for Best Picture and Best Director — James Cameron. Golden Globes are often considered a precursor to the Oscars, so the shift seemed to be moving from *LA Confidential* to *Titanic* once and for all.

On the morning of February 11, the Academy Award nominations were announced, taking everyone by surprise once again. *Titanic* was nominated for a record-tying fourteen Oscars. The nomination that would have set the record for the movie was one for Best Screenplay. But that was not on the list, which proves that sometimes, the nominations are as they should be. (The screenplay is wonderfully readable, but it is clearly a weak aspect of the movie.) In 1950, *All About Eve* was also nominated for fourteen Oscars, actually winning six.

It could hardly be imagined by anyone in the movie business that a full three months after its release, *Titanic* would still be Number One at the box-office, where it has been every week since its release. But the weekend of March 13 would be different. That weekend, MGM released *The Man in the Iron Mask* — also starring Leonardo DiCaprio. MGM was clearly hoping that the new hordes of female fans that swooned over DiCaprio in *Titanic*, and then ran out to rent everything he had ever appeared in, would be quick to line up for the newest screen incarnation of young King Leo. MGM's Julia Perry was astounded that she was once again awaiting the box office results to see if her movie would unseat *Titanic* from the Number One position. The DiCaprio factor certainly inspired confidence, and *The Man in the Iron Mask* was an adventurous, spirited movie based on the classic Alexandre Dumas novel that boasted a solid cast including Jeremy Irons,

Gabriel Byrne, Gerard Depardieu, and John Malkovich. By
Monday morning, it was reported that *Titanic* and *The Man
in the Iron Mask* had, in fact, tied, bringing in $17.5 million
each. The actual figures reported to MGM reflected something slightly different — *Titanic*: $18.3 million, *The Man in
the Iron Mask* : $17.8 million. *Titanic* won again as it continued
to steam ahead toward the record set by *ET The Extraterrestrial*
as box-office champ.

March 23, 1998 was a night to remember. The place was the
Shrine Auditorium in Los Angeles. The occasion was the
Seventieth Annual Academy Awards. The hype had finished
and the wait was over. There had been furious discussion of
a swing in the momentum. In September 1997, *LA Confidential*
was being hailed as the movie to beat at the Oscars. Then
Titanic was released and everything changed. But, on the eve
of the presentations, question were being asked. Was *Titanic*
too successful? Would there be a backlash against the billions
of dollars the movie was raking in? Would the voters reward
the kind of risk that Cameron took, the kind of cinematic
bullet that he dodged?

On the morning of Oscar day, the weekend box-office
results were made public and astonishingly, once again, *Titanic*
remained in the Number One spot for the fourteenth straight
week, beating out the thirteen straight weeks at the Number
One position achieved by both *Tootsie* in 1982 and *Beverly Hills
Cop* in 1984. The film made another $17.3 million and beat

out another set of challengers. Universal Pictures was anxiously anticipating the results of their big release *Primary Colors*, based on the controversial novel by "Anonymous" that detailed the political rise of a philandering, doughnut-eating Southern politician who became president amid a sex scandal. Nikki Rocco, president of distribution at Universal, said, "We knew going in that *Titanic* is a phenomenon and that generally speaking, Oscar-nominated films tend to do well the weekend before the Oscars. So considering what we were up against, I'm perfectly happy we got the silver medal." *Primary Colors* made a healthy $12.4 million. Third place was held down by *Man in the Iron Mask*, which continued to draw in legions of girls who, according to exit polls, "would see anything Leonardo [DiCaprio] was in."

The Academy Awards evening began with the customary walk along the red carpet into the Shrine Auditorium. James Cameron, his then-wife Linda Hamilton, and his parents Shirley and Phillip Cameron forged their way through the media scrum. Linda Hamilton commented that the evening was "the Super Bowl of the film business. A Cinderella-like evening." Perhaps more interesting, though, was her statement that this Academy Awards evening was the "… last hurrah. After the Oscars, we don't even want to say *Titanic* for a long time." When asked about her husband, she responded with a beaming smile, "He's my hero. He's the hardest-working man I have ever seen." Cameron, joining his wife, described himself as "very happy — happy to be a part of this madness."

He was cool but did seem somewhat overwhelmed in his own controlled kind of way. "This kind of glitz and glamour — when you are standing outside looking, you think about how much fun it must be to be a part of it. It really is a magical thing."

From the moment host Billy Crystal took the stage, the gush of *Titanic* jokes and sight gags was unleashed. "Here we are on the *Titanic* — big, expensive, and everyone wants it to go faster." Cuba Gooding Jr. presented the first award of the evening. The statue for Best Supporting Actress went to Kim Bassinger for *LA Confidential*. Gloria Stuart being passed over meant the chances of *Titanic* breaking the *Ben-Hur* record of eleven Oscars were slim. The second Oscar was for Best Costume Design, and with this award, the *Titanic* floodgates opened wide. Deborah Scott took the prize, thanking James Cameron for the "first-class passage." In a hilarious bit of business, Arnold Schwarzenegger introduced a montage of film clips taken from his friend James Cameron's movie. "*Titanic* may gross so much money, no accountant in Hollywood will be able to hide it." He talked about the films on which he worked with Cameron — *The Terminator, Terminator 2: Judgment Day*, and *True Lies* — "back in Jim's art-house days." After Robin Williams won the Oscar for Best Supporting Actor for his role in *Good Will Hunting, Titanic* took the next three Oscars in a row — for Best Sound, Best Sound Effects Editing, and Best Visual Effects. A bit later, James Horner was awarded Best Dramatic Score Oscar. A delighted, but perhaps not entirely surprised, Horner took the stage and thanked Cameron for allowing him to be a part of the history-making project.

James Cameron's first appearance on stage was to receive the Award for Best Editing, which he shared with Conrad Buff. Cameron held his Oscar high and spoke to his daughter Josephine who was watching the ceremony on television, "This is the thing I described to you, the Oscar. It is a really cool thing to get." Then, Céline Dion gave a live performance of "My Heart Will Go On" while wearing the $4-million replica of the heart of the ocean pendant from the movie. She wore a stunning, form-fitting dress, designed specially to complement the stone. After the performance, James Horner accepted his second Oscar of the night for Best Song, thanked Cameron "for being in a good mood the day I brought you this song."

The Oscar darlings of that night, Ben Affleck and Matt Damon, who would win the Best Original Screenplay Oscar for *Good Will Hunting*, took the stage to present the Oscars in the Long and Short Documentary categories. Affleck couldn't resist an ad lib. "This is the one award that I guarantee will not go to Jim Cameron tonight," he said. *Titanic* then won a richly deserved Oscar for Art Direction. Considering the great detail with which the great ship was literally re-created, both inside and out, not winning this award would have been a surprise. Big Daddy Jack Nicholson won the Best Actor Oscar next for his performance as an obsessive compulsive in *As Good As It Gets*, marking his third Oscar in three decades. Even he, the King of Cool, couldn't resist a *Titanic* reference. "I've had this sinking feeling all night..." he began, upon accepting his statue. The next win for *Titanic* came in the Best Cinematography category, which was somewhat of a surprise considering the films it was up against, including Scorcese's shamefully ignored masterpiece *Kundun*.

Now well into the third hour of the ceremony, there were only two Oscars left to present: Best Director and Best Picture. When Warren Beatty announced "... and the Oscar for Best Director goes to ... James Cameron for *Titanic*," Cameron warmly embraced his wife, accepted congratulations from Arnold Schwarzenegger sitting a few rows in front of him, and then bounded onto the stage for the first of two rather strange acceptance speeches. "I don't know about you, but I'm having a really good time," Having thanked his brother Mike for all his help and his assistant director Josh McLaglen, he acknowledged his wife and children and thanked his parents directly, saying, "There is no way I can express what I am feeling in my heart at this moment." Then, thrusting his arms in the air, he yelled, "I'm the king of the world!" in the same way Leonardo DiCaprio's character did aboard the ship as it left port.

The Oscar for Best Picture — the grand finale. Sean Connery presented the award to James Cameron and Jon Landau for *Titanic* to the surprise of no one in the Shrine Auditorium or anywhere in the world watching the event on television. James Cameron took center stage again. "We are here to celebrate the magic of motion pictures and I feel privileged to be a part of that magic," he said. Somberly pointing out that *Titanic* was based on a tragic event during which a staggering number of lives were lost, Cameron called for a moment's silence to honor the dead. He urged the gathered Hollywood glitterati to "listen to the sound of their own hearts, for that which is the most important thing of all." Once he felt the silence had gone on long enough, he stepped to the microphone and said, "Okay, now let's go out and party till dawn."

When it was all said and done, *Titanic* had taken eleven Oscars, tying the record for most Oscars in a single year set by *Ben-Hur* in 1959. James Cameron himself accepted three Oscars for his own contributions. Looking into his eyes, you could see the entire history of this project — the risk, the cost overruns, the difficulties, the size, the delays, the doubts. His eyes made a statement more profound than any issued verbally. They said, "I did it, I really did it. And I did it my way, without compromise."

In the wake of this gargantuan success, arrangements were made to actually pay Cameron for his work on *Titanic*. Statements came forth that the two studios involved would settled with Cameron, to the tune of $100 million. Early reports, which were sketchy and subject to Cameron's approval, listed that figure as a lump-sum amount that would buy Cameron out of any further financial participation in the movie whether it be video-cassette sales or any other ancillary licenses not yet thought of. What was truly mind-warping was that a staggering figure like $100 million represented less than 7 percent of what the film would eventually haul in, *and* it would actually be considerably less than what Cameron was contractually obligated to receive before the giveback — by perhaps as much as $50 million. That's Hollywood.

What does all this mean for James Cameron? What is next for "the King of the World?"

Well, on a personal level, after the marathon publicity commitments were met, Cameron couldn't think much further beyond taking his wife Linda Hamilton on a long overdue honeymoon (they married during the summer of 1997), and spending some quality time with the couple's young daughter Josephine (the Camerons also have a son, Dalton, from Hamilton's first marriage). But on a professional level, the response from Hollywood has been contradictory — everything from "he could write his own ticket" to "I wouldn't want to be the studio that works with him on his next movie." Indeed, how could any studio executive now tell James Cameron that he was wrong about audience expectations or about the worth of risking great sums of money on a film?

One thing that Cameron has wanted to do for years — and now, given the success of *Titanic*, may be allowed to do — is a big-screen version of *Spiderman*. He has said that he wanted it to be his directorial follow-up to *Titanic*, even though it may not be the next movie that bears his name. Seven years ago, Cameron enthusiastically pitched the project to his *Terminator 2: Judgment Day* partners at Carolco Pictures. He

had been interested in bringing the story of journalist Peter
Parker and his transformation into the web-spinning arach-
nid to the big screen for some time, but the cinematic technology either didn't exist or was far too costly to allow him to
make the film to the standard he felt it deserved. After the
leaps and bounds that he made technologywise in *Terminator 2*,
he then felt it was possible to create *Spiderman*. Carolco
agreed. They agreed to the tune of $5 million, the amount
they fronted to develop it. But the project was blindsided by
legal challenges over the exact ownership of the screen rights
to the comic book. When Carolco went bust in 1992, Twentieth
Century Fox stepped in and tried to buy the rights specifically
for Cameron. However, they found that in the Carolco bankruptcy proceedings, the screen rights to *Spiderman* had been
transferred to MGM/UA. MGM/UA had stated they were
partnered with an independent production company — Twenty-
First Century Films — and they had clear ownership to the
rights. Then, media giant Viacom claimed *they* controlled the
rights to *Spiderman*, or at least the first refusal rights, with
Columbia Tri-Star Home Video claiming they controlled the
video rights. Twentieth Century Fox was still interested in
obtaining the property, but it would cost them big. Another
scenario saw Fox partnering with the owners in a coproduc-
tion arrangement (it certainly worked with *Titanic*.) Just as the
situation seemed to be coming close to some resolution, Marvel
Comics found itself in bankruptcy court. In June 1998, a medi-
ation hearing was scheduled in Los Angeles to settle the matter

once and for all. In the meantime Cameron was also discussing another project that was of special interest (and presumably less of a headache) to him — a remake of the science-fiction classic *Planet of the Apes*.

As "King of the World," Cameron is now taking the opportunity to answer some of his critics from the lofty perch on which he now finds himself. Throughout the making of *Titanic*, Kenneth Turan, the highly respected journalist for the *Los Angeles Times*, was hardly a supporter of Cameron and the movie. When the film was released, Turan's review was one of the few that dared to point out the obvious shortcomings in the movie, but in a balanced way. He then continued to write and commentate on the success of the *Titanic* in a very negative way. This culminated with a scathing article printed in the March 21, 1998 edition of the *Los Angeles Times* entitled "You Try to Stop It" in which Turan opined that the success of *Titanic* actually did more to point out the weaknesses of modern-day movies than a newfound strength in writing and that the *Titanic* script was so bad, "it almost makes you weep in frustration."

Cameron took the opportunity to write a rather scathing criticism of his own aimed at Kenneth Turan in the form of a letter to the editor. Remarkably, the *Los Angeles Times* printed the 1300-word letter in its entirety in the March 28, 1998 edition, featuring a portion of it on the page of the Calender section of the Saturday edition. This touched off a wave of responses from people taking either Turan's or Cameron's side.

The *Los Angeles Times* reported having received over one hundred phone calls, letters, e-mails, and faxes — considered the largest response to any story they can ever remember. The responses were divided 59 percent in favor of Cameron, 39 percent in favor of Turan, and 2 percent pretty much on the fence.

The Oscar wins and the headlines have turned James Cameron, already a controversial figure in the movie world, into a bona fide celebrity. Witness the attention he received leading up to the Oscars — a full-page ad taken out by American Express in glossy entertainment and lifestyle magazines featured his card prominently among the cards of other much more recognizable movie stars. Keep flipping the pages and you would have come to a full-page ad sponsored by something known as the National Fluid Milk Processor Promotion Board. The ad featured James Cameron standing in front of his huge *Titanic* model with a milk mustache. The caption read, "I like to float big chunks of ice in mine."

In the midst of this self-congratulatory fervor, Cameron could still show the real reason he did this stuff, the real reason he made this movie and what it actually meant to him. When asked if he had any regrets about this project he became thoughtful for a moment, then described his sadness at seeing the glorious sets he had built for the movie being dismantled. To him, they were "beautiful" and the realization that these gorgeous re-creations would not exist any more profoundly saddened him. Cameron restored the glory that *Titanic* had when she was first built, and he was very proud of that accomplishment.

It was a mathematical certainty that eventually *Titanic* would be knocked from the Number One spot at the box office. On April 6, 1998, the box-office numbers had science fiction remake of the 1960s TV show *Lost in Space* earning $20.5 million to *Titanic*'s $11.6 million. *Titanic*'s wave of success had crested at fifteen straight weeks, narrowly missing the record of eighteen weeks set by *ET The Extraterrestrial* in 1982.

On April 10, 1998, *Titanic* opened in what is potentially the most lucrative of all markets on earth — China. The movie hit the ground running, with an endorsement from no less than President Jiang Zemin. But the reaction was mixed.

The *China News Service* was on top of the story. "People who like the movie say they mainly appreciate its sad and beautiful love story, stirring scenes, huge production, and moving music. People who are disappointed say the story is very old, the performances are clumsy, there are problems with the plot, and there is not much food for thought."

President Ziang, the leader or the Chinese Communist Party, was quite enthusiastic in his description of *Titanic*. When told that the movie was made for $200 million and had brought in, to date, over $1.2 billion, President Jiang chuckled, "That's venture capital, eh?"

Like everywhere else, street vendors in China were cleaning up, selling everything they could with images from *Titanic* on them, including watches with Jack and Rose on the face.

Curiously, one poster for *Titanic* on a Beijing street featured images of Leonardo DiCaprio and Kate Winslet looking into each others eyes and smiling. The ship was not featured at all.

What continues to be fascinating and telling was the reaction to this movie the world over — fifty-six countries besides the United States as of late April 1998. The Russian premiere of the movie was held in mid-February in Kaliningrad. James Cameron attended and spoke to the assembled crowd beforehand. Kaliningrad, on the Baltic Sea, is the home of the oceanographic institute that houses the Mir submersibles Cameron found indispensable during his research and making of the movie. For this premiere, Cameron arranged for almost three tons of sound equipment to be shipped to the Zarya theater in Kaliningrad so that it could be updated in order to maximize the enjoyment for his Russian viewers.

In Russia, movie audiences have been reacting very strongly indeed. Irina Valova, the marketing director of the Kodak Kinomir, a theater that showed *Titanic* exclusively for over a month, described the Russian audiences as "very soulful" and that "many needed a couple of days to recover from the tragedy." The theater was packed showing after showing even though the price of a ticket was 100 rubles ($18) — twice the regular admission price.

In Japan, where the world premiere of the movie took place, the reaction had been the hardest to read. The movie had several characters that exhibited a character trait the Japanese call "gamen" — which can be translated into the ability to remain strong in the face of extreme adversity. But from the standpoint of critical analysis, the reaction to the movie was somewhat mixed. Nagaharu Yodagawa, a leading film critic in Japan, found the movie to be blatantly commercial, writing "It is spectacular but full of reminders that the producer does not want the movie to fail financially."

In Britain, *Titanic* held a special meaning and was received warmly for the most part, but there was some strong sentiment in the cautionary words written by *The Guardian's* Michael Freedland: "James Cameron may think he is king of the world, but he could turn out to be a monarch of a new kind of hell, presiding over what could be the worst time in Hollywood history."

This notion of American moviemakers and their apparent willingness to buy success at any cost was also shared by the critics in France, where moviemaking in considered a serious art form. But even these French writers and intellectuals, who usually arbitrarily dismiss anything that comes out of Hollywood, found reasons to endorse *Titanic*. Serge July wrote in *Libération*, "The subject of the film is not — this is obvious — the sinking of the famous ship, but the suicide in the middle of the Atlantic of a society divided in classes." Didier Peron, who also wrote for *Libération*, stated, "*Titanic* is a politically committed film."

The people of Dalbeattie, Scotland complained about Cameron's mistreatment of the character of First Officer Murdoch. But the people of France sang Cameron's praise for pointing out that the ship made a stop at the French port of Cherbourg where 274 passengers, plus a number of French domestic servants who were not registered as passengers (so their passing was never officially acknowledged), boarded the ill-fated liner.

India claims to have the largest moviegoing audience in the world. *Titanic* played, in English, to over two million people in five weeks. Many of the audience members understood little or no English. Shavran Shroff, spokesman for the largest theater chain in India, said, "*Titanic* will be presented in English as long as there is an audience to see it — then it will be released in Hindi and other vernacular languages later in the year."

In Turkey, *Titanic* drew in 26,000 patrons each day during its first five weeks in release, overtaking the current holder of the Turkish attendance record, *Bandit*, from filmmaker Mine Vargi. Vargi's film was nominated for Best Foreign Language Film at the 1998 Academy Awards. He reacted to the success of *Titanic* this way: "Simply, Turks are very sentimental people, and *Titanic* appeals to that."

In Egypt, the movie was sold out for weeks in advance. A prominent film critic in Cairo, Khaled Farahat, said, "This is not an American movie, it is a *human* movie." A simple reaction explains it all.

By early April 1998, over fourteen million Germans had laid down their Deutschmarks to see *Titanic*. There, too, DiCaprio was drawing in the teenage girls, but older, more sophisticated viewers were again dissecting the movie in the loftiest of terms. National magazines like *Die Zeit* and *Der*

Spiegel described the movie as a symbol that provided cathar-
sis for all, a surrogate myth in a trivialized era, an icon of the
end of history.

Part of the enormous resonating report from the great
Titanic cannon blast was the very public dissolution of Cameron's
nine-month marriage (his fourth in total) to actress Linda
Hamilton. The strain of making *Titanic* probably should be
taken into account, as could the fact that Cameron had an obvious crush on *Titanic* costar Suzy Amis during the Halifax leg
of the shooting. After the Oscar ceremony, Hamilton was asked
if the Oscar haul would have an effect on her husband one
way or the other. She responded curtly, "He was always a jerk,
so there's no way to really measure."

Another by-product is that brand of celebrity usually
reserved for big-screen actors. On the 1998 season finale of
the hit sitcom *Mad About You*, Cameron made a comedic cameo
appearance opposite the star of the show, Paul Reiser, who
played a small time New York filmmaker in the series.

Throughout the Titanic experience, Canada remained
heartily interested in its billion-dollar native son. In the summer of 1998, James Cameron visited the Niagara Falls Film
Festival, a showing of the old and the new that focused more
on camp than on quality. There, he unveiled a 70-mm print
of *Titanic*, to be shown on a huge IMAX screen. Another
water-based entry in the festival was the terrific Irwin Allen
disaster movie that was also a major success in its day — *The
Poseidon Adventure*.

In June 1998, Cameron received an honorary doctorate from Ottawa's Carleton University and an honorary degree from Ryerson Polytechnical University. Carleton named Cameron a Doctor of Fine Arts, "in recognition of his distinguished career as a Canadian filmmaker." Wags and detractors immediately set upon this statement like a pack of hungry hyenas. This, they maintained, was another example of a Canadian having triumphed in the American system before being recognized and honored in Canada. There was also a bit of snickering involved in handing a Doctorate of Fine Arts to the guy behind *Rambo: First Blood Part 2*, *The Terminator* films, and *Piranha 2: The Spawning*.

The previously unprecedented success of *Titanic* has made one thing perfectly clear. James Cameron, the kid from Kapuskasing, Ontario, showed the world that there *is* great reward in having the guts to dream big — and dream aloud.

A James Cameron

FILMOGRAPHY

Battle Beyond the Stars

1980

104 minutes

A planet under siege hires interplanetary mercenaries to help repel an armada of malevolent invaders bent on domination. John Sayles fashioned the script for this amusing science fiction movie after Kurosawa's *The Seven Samurai.*

PRODUCER: Roger Corman
DIRECTOR: Jimmy T. Murakami
WRITER: John Sayles
CINEMATOGRAPHER: Daniel Lacambre
ART DIRECTORS: James Cameron, Charles Breen
CAST: Richard Thomas, Robert Vaughn, John Saxon, Sybil Danning,
    George Peppard, Sam Jaffe

Escape from New York

1981

99 minutes

Manhattan has been turned into a maximum-security prison. A plane carrying the president of the United States crashes on the island and the president is taken hostage. A war hero ex-con is engaged to go in and rescue him. This wildly inventive film makes the viewer mourn the death of the B-movie. On a $3.5-million budget Carpenter *et al.* achieved a visually satisfying film using ingenuity and skill.

PRODUCERS: Larry Franco, Debra Hill
DIRECTOR: John Carpenter
WRITERS: John Carpenter, Nick Castle
CINEMATOGRAPHER: Dean Cundey
MATTE ARTWORK & SPECIAL EFFECTS DIRECTOR OF PHOTOGRAPHY:
    James Cameron
CAST: Kurt Russell, Lee Van Cleef, Ernest Borgnine, Donald
    Pleasence, Isaac Hayes, Adrienne Barbeau, Harry Dean Stanton

Galaxy of Terror

1981
85 minutes

An abjectly silly science fiction movie and low-rent ripoff of *Alien*, about a group of space explorers who travel to a planet where every horror they imagine in their minds becomes reality. The effects are inventive though nauseating, but the movie is entirely forgettable.

PRODUCER: Roger Corman
DIRECTOR: Bruce Clark
WRITERS: Mark Siegler, Bruce Clark
PRODUCTION DESIGNER: James Cameron
CAST: Edward Albert, Erin Moran, Ray Walston

Piranha 2: The Spawning aka Piranha 2: Flying Killers

1982
94 minutes

Vacationers at a seaside resort in the Caribbean are suddenly attacked by a school of mutated flying piranha fish in this laughable horror flick.

The sequel to a witty little horror movie called *Piranha* (1978) written by John Sayles and directed with style and humor by Joe Dante, two assets visibly lacking in this film.

PRODUCERS: Chako van Leevwew, Jeff Schechtman
DIRECTOR: James Cameron
WRITER: H. A. Milton
CINEMATOGRAPHER: Roberto D'Ettore
MUSIC: Steve Powder
CAST: Lance Henriksen, Patricia O'Neil, Steve Marachuk, Ricky Paul, Ted Richert, Leslie Graves

Android

1982

80 minutes

It's 2036 and an almost human android has been working as an assistant to a mad scientist, played with his usual panache by Klaus Kinski. The android, MAX 404, demands vengeance when he learns he is about to be decommissioned. MAX is played by Don Opper, who also wrote the screenplay.

PRODUCER: Mary Ann Fisher
DIRECTOR: Aaron Lipstadt
WRITERS: Don Opper, James Reigle
CINEMATOGRAPHER: Tim Suhrstedt
MUSIC: Don Preston
DESIGN CONSULTANT: James Cameron
CAST: Klaus Kinski, Brie Howard, Norbert Weisser, Crofton Hardester, Kendra Kirchner, Don Opper

The Terminator

1984

108 minutes

A cyborg is sent back from the future on a mission to prevent the birth of a young man who will grow into a powerful resistance forces leader in a future war. The Terminator's target, the young mother to be, has a protector, also sent from the future, in the form of a soldier named Reese. He and the Terminator battle it out while the future of mankind hangs in the balance.

PRODUCER: Gale Anne Hurd

DIRECTOR: James Cameron

WRITERS: James Cameron, Gale Anne Hurd

CINEMATOGRAPHER: Adam Greenberg

MUSIC: Brad Feidel

CAST: Arnold Schwarzenegger, Michael Biehn, Linda Hamilton, Paul Winfield, Rick Rossovich, Lance Henriksen

Rambo: First Blood Part II

1985

92 minutes

Former Green Beret John Rambo is serving time in prison for his misadventures in the first *Rambo* movie, *First Blood*. He is released through the machinations of his old colonel to lead a mission to Vietnam to rescue some forgotten POWs.

PRODUCER: Buzz Feitshans

DIRECTOR: George Pan Cosmatos

WRITERS: Sylvester Stallone, James Cameron

CINEMATOGRAPHER: Jack Cardiff

MUSIC: Jerry Goldsmith

CAST: Sylvester Stallone, Richard Crenna, Charles Napier, Julia
  Nickson, Steven Berkoff

Aliens

1986
137 minutes

Ripley, the sole survivor of a team of space mining engineers, is found
floating in space in suspended animation. She is asked to join a mission
back to the planet filled with horrific aliens that killed her crewmates
in *Alien* (1979). This movie was one of the biggest hits of the year and
earned seven Oscar nominations.

PRODUCER: Gale Anne Hurd
DIRECTOR: James Cameron
WRITERS: James Cameron, Walter Hill, David Giler
CINEMATOGRAPHER: Adrian Biddle
MUSIC: James Horner
CAST: Sigourney Weaver, Michael Biehn, Carrie Henn, Bill Paxton,
  Paul Reiser
ACADEMY AWARDS: Best Visual Effects, Best Sound Effects Editing
ACADEMY AWARD NOMINATIONS: Best Actress (Weaver), Best Art
  Direction/Set Direction, Best Film Editing, Best Sound, Best
  Original Score

Alien Nation

1988
94 minutes

Alien drug-smuggling refugees from another planet make their way to
Earth and are assimilated into human society. The idea behind this
movie was intriguing but it ended up a routine cops-and-robbers action
flick.

PRODUCERS: Gale Anne Hurd, Richard Kobritz
DIRECTOR: Graham Baker
WRITER: Rockne S. O'Bannon (uncredited rewrite by James Cameron)
CINEMATOGRAPHER: Adam Greenberg
MUSIC: Curt Sobel
CAST: James Caan, Mandy Patinkin, Terence Stam

The Abyss

1989
140 minutes

After an unknown entity sinks an American atomic submarine, an undersea oil rig is sent to attempt a rescue. The oil riggers and the rescue team encounter a civilization living deep in an ocean trough. A visually dazzling movie filmed under the most demanding of technical conditions.

PRODUCER: Gale Anne Hurd
DIRECTOR: James Cameron
WRITER: James Cameron
CINEMATOGRAPHER: Mikael Salomon
MUSIC: Alan Silvestri
CAST: Ed Harris, Mary Elizabeth Mastrantonio, Michael Biehn, Leo
    Burmester, Todd Graff
ACADEMY AWARD: Best Visual Effects
ACADEMY AWARD NOMINATIONS: Best Cinematography, Best Art
    Direction, Best Sound

Point Break

1991
117 minutes

A group of surfers finance their lifestyle with bank robbery and are the target of an FBI infiltration investigation.

EXECUTIVE PRODUCER: James Cameron
PRODUCERS: Peter Abrams, Mike Levy
DIRECTOR: Kathryn Bigelow
WRITER: W. Peter Illif (uncredited rewrite by James Cameron)
CINEMATOGRAPHER: Donald Peterman
MUSIC: Mark Isham
CAST: Patrick Swayze, Keanu Reeves, Gary Busey, James LeGros,
Bojesse Christopher, John C. McGinley
MTV MOVIE AWARD: Most Desirable Male (Reeves)

Terminator 2: Judgment Day

1991

135 minutes

The Terminator is back, this time to protect the child whose birth the
original Terminator tried to prevent. A high-tech thrill-a-minute movie
that pushed the boundaries of cinematic technology.

PRODUCER: James Cameron
DIRECTOR: James Cameron
WRITERS: James Cameron, William Wisher
CINEMATOGRAPHER: Adam Greenberg
MUSIC: Brad Fiedel
CAST: Arnold Schwarzenegger, Linda Hamilton, Edward Furlong,
Robert Patrick, Joe Morton
ACADEMY AWARDS: Best Makeup, Best Sound,
Best Sound Effects Editing, Best Visual Effects
ACADEMY AWARD NOMINATION: Best Cinematography
MTV MOVIE AWARDS: Best Film, Best Male Performance
(Schwarzenegger), Best Female Performance (Hamilton), Break-
through Performance (Furlong), Most Desirable Female
(Hamilton), Best Action Sequence
PEOPLE'S CHOICE AWARD: Best Film

True Lies

1994

141 minutes

A big-budget remake of a little-known French farce about the double life of a secret agent. Dazzling stunts and set pieces abound amid the domestic comedy and lighthearted spy plot.

PRODUCERS: James Cameron, Stephanie Austin
DIRECTOR: James Cameron
WRITER: James Cameron
CINEMATOGRAPHER: Russell Carpenter
MUSIC: Brad Fiedel
CAST: Arnold Schwarzenegger, Jamie Lee Curtis, Tom Arnold, Bill
    Paxton, Tia Carrere, Art Malik, Charlton Heston
ACADEMY AWARD NOMINATION: Best Visual Effects
GOLDEN GLOBE AWARD: Best Actress — Musical/Comedy (Curtis)
MTV MOVIE AWARD NOMINATIONS: Best Female Performance
    (Curtis), Best Action Sequence, Best Dance Sequence
    (Schwarzenegger/Carrere)

Strange Days

1995

145 minutes

New Year's Eve 1999 is the setting for this thriller about ex-cop Lenny Nero who deals underground data-discs containing recorded memories and emotions.

PRODUCERS: James Cameron, Steven Charles Jaffe
DIRECTOR: Kathryn Bigelow
WRITERS: James Cameron, Jay Cocks
CINEMATOGRAPHER: Matthew Leonetti

MUSIC: Graeme Revell
CAST: Ralph Fiennes, Juliette Lewis, Angela Bassett, Tom Sizemore, Michael Wincott

Titanic

1997

197 minutes

A poignant love story set against the sinking of the luxury liner RMS *Titanic* on April 15, 1912. The movie is book-ended by a modern-day story of a treasure hunter searching the wreck of the *Titanic* in search of a priceless necklace.

PRODUCERS: James Cameron, Jon Landau
DIRECTOR: James Cameron
WRITER: James Cameron
CINEMATOGRAPHER: Russell Carpenter
MUSIC: James Horner
CAST: Leonardo DiCaprio, Kate Winslet, Billy Zane, Kathy Bates, Frances Fisher, Gloria Stuart, Bernard Hill, and Bill Paxton
ACADEMY AWARDS: Best Picture, Best Director, Best Editing, Best Cinematography, Best Art Direction, Best Dramatic Musical Score, Best Original Song ("My Heart Will Go On"), Best Visual Effects, Best Costumes, Best Sound, Best Sound Effects Editing
ALSO NOMINATED FOR: Best Actress, Best Supporting Actress, and Best Makeup Effects.

SOURCES

Books

Andrews, Nigel. *True Myths: The Life and Times of Arnold Schwarzenegger.* London: Bloomsbury Books, 1996.

Cameron, James. *Strange Days.* New York: Plume Paperbacks, 1995.

Cameron, James, and Wisher, William. *Terminator 2: Judgment Day: The Book of the Film.* New York: Applause Theatre Books, 1991.

Hunter, Stephen. *Violent Screen: A Critic's 13 Years on the Front Lines of Movie Mayhem.* New York: Doubleday, 1997.

Kael, Pauline. *For Keeps.* New York: E.P. Dutton, 1994.

Schanzer, Karl, and Wright, Thomas Lee. *American Screenwriters.* New York: Avon Books, 1993.

Magazines

Benedict, Jennifer. "The Terminator," *Cinefex*, issue 21.

Davidson, Jody. "A Once and Future War," *Cinefex*, issue 47.

Richardson, John R. "Iron Jim," *Premiere*, August 1994.

Shay, Don. "Aliens," *Cinefex*, issue 27.

ibid. "Dancing on the Edge of the Abyss," *Cinefex*, issue 39.

ibid. "True Lies," *Cinefex*, issue 59.

Shay, Estelle. "T2 3-D Battle Across Time," *Cinefex*, issue 68.

INDEX